WAL

Everything I've Ever Learned About Change

Please visit Hay House UK: www.hayhouse.co.uk;
Hay House USA: www.hayhouse.com;
Hay House Australia: www.hayhouse.com.au;
Hay House South Africa: orders@psdprom.co.za

Everything I've Ever Learned About Change

Lesley Garner

HAY HOUSE

Australia • Canada • Hong Kong
South Africa • United Kingdom • United States

First published and distributed in the United Kingdom by:
Hay House UK Ltd, 292B Kensal Rd, London W10 5BE.
Tel.: (44) 20 8962 1230; Fax: (44) 20 8962 1239. www.hayhouse.co.uk

Published and distributed in the United States of America by:
Hay House, Inc., PO Box 5100, Carlsbad, CA 92018-5100.
Tel.: (1) 760 431 7695 or (800) 654 5126; Fax (1) 760 431 6948 or (800) 650 5115. www.hayhouse.com

Published and distributed in Australia by:
Hay House Australia Ltd, 18/36 Ralph St, Alexandria NSW 2015.
Tel.: (61) 2 9669 4299; Fax: (61) 2 9669 4144. www.hayhouse.com.au

Published and distributed in the Republic of South Africa by:
Hay House SA (Pty), Ltd, PO Box 990, Witkoppen 2068.
Tel./Fax: (27) 11 706 6612. orders@psdprom.co.za

Distributed in Canada by:
Raincoast, 9050 Shaughnessy St, Vancouver, BC V6P 6E5.
Tel.: (1) 604 323 7100; Fax: (1) 604 323 2600

Cover design by Leanne Siu
Interior design by e-Digital Design
Edited by Lizzie Hutchins

08 07 06 05 04   5 4 3 2 1

A catalogue record for this book is available from the British Library.

ISBN 1-4019-1104-8
ISBN 978-1-4019-1104-1

Printed and bound in Great Britain by TJ International, Padstow, Cornwall.

This book is for my daughters, Harriet and Rachel, who changed my life immeasurably for the better. May this book be of some help in all the changes that lie ahead of you.

Contents

Acknowledgements

There is an unseen army of friends, family and colleagues who have accompanied me through all the changes in my life and even precipitated some of them. You know who you are and I hope you know how much I've appreciated your friendship and advice. I can't mention everyone here, but I have to mention a few, especially Ken Grant, the man who changed my life the most by whisking me off to Ethiopia and Afghanistan, marrying me and giving me two children. The marriage might not have lasted, but the friendship has, and Ken is a remarkable example of someone who is always solving problems, thinking laterally and staying one step ahead of everyone else.

In contrast, my friend David Braybrook is a model of calm and I find his Quaker ways very soothing when my own life is too hectic. I thank him for explaining Quaker practice to me, and I thank him and his partner, Daryl Morton, for offering me welcome and shelter in their peaceful home.

I am grateful to Roger McGough for giving me permission to quote from his poem 'I am not Sleeping', from the Penguin edition of his *Selected Poems*.

Cameron Greig has gone home to New Zealand and I haven't seen him since our day out in Paris, but I hope he remembers it as fondly as I do. He was good company.

Thank you to the members of the Funding Network and the many applicants for their funds for showing me how many ways there are of changing the world for the better.

And thank you to my friend Caroline Mustill for taking me along to the Royal Albert Hall to meet Sir Harrison Birtwistle and attend his rehearsal, and for many other jolly outings and good conversations besides.

Thank you, of course, to Marianna Alexander, my Samurai partner, and to that group of friends who met through the Actors' Institute and who are still, in various ways, committed to creative change. Here's to pathfinding our way through life together when we are in our eighties and nineties and beyond.

How to Use This Book

Change is inevitable. Nothing stays still. Life is in constant motion from the molecular to the planetary level and we are changing right along with it. The universe moves in a perpetual surging dance, and happiness is the elation that comes from feeling in harmony with that cosmic rhythm.

So why is change the source of so much fear and unhappiness? Why do people resist it so deeply and struggle against it so desperately? Why, if change is the norm, do we all recognize the profound longing for eternal sameness? 'Change and decay in all around I see,' sing the mourners at a funeral. 'O thou that changeth not, abide with me.'

We long for sameness. But if we could arrest change and enter a world of eternal stasis we would go mad. We would stagnate and die, because change is life. Constant adaptation creates the momentum and energy that keep us going.

Our relationship with and understanding of the forces of change within us and around us, both personal and political, are crucial to our wellbeing. Without some surrender to change and understanding of its role in our life, we suffer.

Life gives us endless chances to learn about change. One minute life is stuck, the next minute it is out of control and moving at headlong speed. When life is stuck, we long to make changes. When life is out of control, we long for things to stay the same.

If we can stay aware, we will notice that there are two kinds of changes: those that happen to us and those that we make happen. It is very important to understand the difference. The more of the second kind there are in your life, the happier you will be, so this book celebrates the exhilaration of change.

However, the art of dealing with change when it happens to you is also essential to happiness. A human life is a never-ending lesson in adjusting to change: biological, hormonal, familial, changes of home or relationship, changes of mind and heart, changes of fortune and circumstance, changes of government and climate. A single life can encompass peaceful democracy and war, a perfect sunny day or a hurricane, the slow morphing of evolution or the cataclysm of a tsunami. Change can flatten you or teach you to be adaptable, resourceful and even triumphant. That is what this book is about.

So, faced with the inevitable changes of life, what can we do? We can do a lot. We can understand the forces that affect us and be better prepared. We can learn to read the writing on the wall in relationships, in workplaces and in nations. We can learn the arts of adaptation, self-preservation and creative living. We can learn how to nourish ourselves and anchor ourselves in those aspects of life that change more slowly than we do and give us glimpses of the eternal. And we can learn how to empower ourselves by becoming an agent of change. Change isn't something we have to suffer. It can be something we work to bring about.

In this book I give many techniques for dealing with change, some drawn from my own life, some from the experiences and skills of others. You don't have to read it in any order. The chapters are meditations on different aspects of change, not sets of rules, and I hope they will stimulate your own thinking rather than replace it. Whether you are desperately stuck in the mud or being swept away in the current of your life, I hope there are ideas here that will get you riding the inevitable, interminable waves, ideas that will even have you enjoying a thrilling ride.

Introduction

The idea for a book about change came to me when I realized that it was all anybody ever talked about. It was a theme that blew like an invisible wind through every conversation. The weather wasn't like this last year. Someone's delightful child has suddenly become a rude teenager. Someone else had finished a project and didn't know what to do next. This person had found a new house. That person had just been fired. This person had found the love of their life on the internet and was moving to another country. That person was setting up a new company, undergoing a religious conversion, dealing with bereavement, campaigning against poverty...

Everyone wanted change, hated change, was challenged by change, was dealing, in one way or another, with change. There was no avoiding it.

As for me, in one year I had published a book, moved house twice and watched my father die. The practical changes demanded by these major events involved the daily making of lists, the clearing out of a family house and the hunting for a new home, plus the organizing of removal vans, storage and a funeral. These activities were simply the outward manifestations of inward seismic shifts. My identity, my place in the family, my address, my habitual ways of relating to the world and my geographical base were all being upended. I could go from extreme misery to elation in a single day. No wonder that some nights I couldn't sleep. No wonder that some days I couldn't remember the simplest things, like where I'd put my keys.

I am old enough to know that this is the way it is, especially if change comes faster than you can deal with it. I know that in time I will adapt and survive and what looks like a change for the worse can be turned into one for the better. I know that every loss makes way for something new. Even in the chaos I have a sense of myself that remains true. I have friends who have gone through this before and can help me hold my balance. I have techniques and knowledge and practices that will keep me steady. I have health and therefore I have optimism.

If you are small or old or vulnerable, it can feel very different. Change can disturb you beyond words. I know a little girl who is only four years old. She has moved house, so her whole physical world has shifted. Her family is the same, but her town, her street and her bedroom are not. And she has started at a new school. School is a huge and scary new world. It has rules she doesn't understand and teachers who are very tall and children who are bigger and louder and more confident than she is. She makes two new friends and she likes her class teacher, who is kind to her. But her parents don't like the new school. After a few weeks they find her a new one and she is confronted with one big change too many. She will lose her nice new teacher and her two new friends. She gets asthma.

She – and sometimes all of us, if life moves too fast – is like a small animal lost in the long grass, and she can hardly breathe for the fear. She doesn't know that a lifetime of new schools, moves, new jobs, losses and triumphs, travel, political changes and even wars stretches ahead of her. She doesn't know that a day could come when she will greet yet another change with a thought no more dramatic than 'Here we go again' or 'Well, I've survived before' or even 'New school! Hooray!' She doesn't know that she could become a change junkie, addicted to something on the scale between ordinary restlessness and genuine exploration. She could become a pathfinder, a change agent, a revolutionary. She could become one of those people who see the world in terms of solutions, not problems, and who change the course of medicine or science, politics or the arts. The stronger her own centre and her self-belief, the more easily she will be able not only to ride the waves of change but to make waves of her own. She could be a visionary. She could be a leader. She could change the world.

This book is for her and for everyone like her, for everyone who starts being made breathless by change and ends by taking our breath away.

Back to the Future, Forward to Normal

When I was a little girl I came into a world at peace. That is what the dates will tell you. Actually, I came into a world which was not so much peaceful as exhausted by war. It was a tired, shabby, make-do-and-mend world, a world in which people survived and hoped for some kind of return to normality. It was a world in which people longed to go back to the future.

What I mean by that is that they hoped they could create a future which was something like the better bits of the past. Men and women returned from the war. They jumped into bed together and set up house in the ruins of their former world. The women took off their uniforms and put on aprons. There was a baby boom and I was, and still am, part of that boom, a generation which carried on changing the world in turn. For our parents there were home-making and a longing for stability and, among progressive people, a belief that a brave new modern world could rise out of the ashes of the old. People didn't so much want to go back to normal as look forward to normal.

In a world of constant change, what is normal? Is it something you can take for granted or something that only becomes clear once it has gone? I certainly wouldn't want to go back to the normal of my childhood. Life now is much more exciting. I grew up in a world of repeated, devoutly held certainties, repeated and devoutly held because people longed for them to be true even when they weren't. People met and married and lived happily ever after. It wasn't just the mantra of fairytales. Divorce was very rare. People set up house together and had children. The family gathered round the table together and ate roast meat and vegetables for Sunday lunch. People went to church and worshipped together and stood for the national anthem and prayed for king and country. Women stayed at home and looked after the house and men went to work from nine o'clock to five o'clock and came home and had tea with the family. They hoped that their job was for life. Very few people travelled abroad for pleasure, though millions had been displaced by war and had seen the world by fighting in it.

Britain still had an empire when I was born and even though India won its independence in 1947, by the time I went to school most of the world map on my classroom wall was still coloured pink to show all our possessions and dominions. The royal family went on great long tours of the Commonwealth and we used to go to the cinema and watch the patriotic newsreels that showed them being welcomed by cheering black people around the world, though it was very rare to see a black face on a British street.

Europe was tired. Everything glamorous and fresh seemed to come from America – nylons, lipstick, movie stars and sex.

I think of the world of my childhood as a quiet, ordered, conventional, black-and-white world. Partly this was because of the impoverishment and depletion of the post-war period. Partly this was because I was a child and people simplify the world for children as much as they can. Adults and children collude in wanting the world to be a safe, secure, unchanging place. But it isn't.

As I grew up, things changed. Affluence and technology slowly turned up the volume and the throttle. Television shoved the radio aside. Music became amplified. Vinyl replaced shellac. The very quiet streets where I could walk alone to school and back filled up with traffic. We got our first car. We flew on our first plane. We had our first holiday abroad and so did millions of other people. Now I envy our innocence and inexperience because it meant that we constantly discovered the new and marvellous and had the fresh thrill of achievement.

Everything changes all the time, and faster. If I were to look at a speeded-up film of my life it would be hysterical. The length of my hair and skirts would shoot up and down. People would come and go like a swarm of hyperactive ants. I would whiz from home to home, city to city, country to country. If you could see inside my head, my dreams and thoughts would change at dizzying speed. My hopes, fears, ideas, visions of the future and memories of the past would constantly form and reform like speeded-up film clouds...

And the world around me would transform. My life would unreel as part of a great technological revolution. I would whiz from a world of empty streets, pen and paper, cardboard and string right through to a traffic-clogged computer age where you can cram the whole world onto a microchip and the hills are alive with the sound of mobile phones.

National borders and identities and ideologies would collapse and rise all round me like decks of cards. Enemies and allies would change places. Armies and air forces would zoom round the globe. Communism would collapse and apartheid implode and the Cold War turn warm. Democracy would spread in one direction and Islamic fundamentalism in another. The polar icecaps would begin to melt and forests turn to stubble. And often, at some high-speed turn of events, I would sigh, 'I just want to get back to normal.' But I would still have to keep going forward.

What is normal in all this? What is normal for the refugee who is fleeing the demolition of their known world? What is normal for the family who have suddenly lost a loved member and whose world has fallen apart? What is normal for the person who has suddenly won the lottery or met the love of their life? Great good fortune and happiness can be just as disconcerting as tragedy. They all share the same surreal quality, the same struggle to integrate the new into the old.

Normality is what is repeated until it is taken for granted. It is normal to turn on a switch and get electric light, unless you live in a jungle or a war zone. It is normal to be constantly told you are wonderful if you are a prima donna, or stupid if you are the child of an abusive family. We all have our own normal.

The pace of change in our lives is so fast that the moment comes to all of us, no matter what is going on, when we long to get back to normal. When we realize that what we think of as normal no longer exists, we learn that normal is something we have to create afresh, again and again. There is no 'back to normal' because normal is always changing, but we can go forward. We can design and build our own normality, and therein lies the liberation and the energy of change.

Get Lost

I am very fond of getting lost on purpose. If there's somewhere I haven't been before I want to go there. If there's a part of town I normally skirt, I make myself dive in. If the map says that way I'll go this way, just to see what's there. I'm like G. K. Chesterton's rolling English drunkard who made the rolling English road, and when the poet says 'We went to Paradise by way of Kensal Green,' I don't think, 'Idiots,' I think, 'That sounds like fun.' It's not beer I'm drunk on when I take a left where I normally take a right, just to see where it gets me. It's the exhilaration of a change of view and a remapping of the brain. I know I'm going to learn something.

I'm not pretending that this enforced exploration is always joyous. I lost half an hour just this morning zig-zagging through the unlovely back streets of the east end of my city because I am arrogant about it too and so I was blowed if I was going to stop and look at a map. But that half an hour was an eye-opener. I saw a very different London from the one I normally see. I saw people of all races in the streets and shops and cafés that you don't see even half a mile away. I saw new mosques and old graveyards and restored churches and startling new architecture. My idea of the city I live in reformed itself in my brain as I slowly joined up the unfamiliar bits with the places I knew and I came out triumphantly where I thought I would after all.

So how lost was I really? Is it possible to take the risk of throwing the map away and trying to formulate your journey and your goal in a new way?

The world is full of maps. People talk about their destiny being mapped out. There are maps for education and maps for careers and maps that will take you from birth to death. If you are born rich and privileged, your path is mapped through the right schools and the right marriage to the right position in life. If you are poor and uneducated, you may feel that your life is mapped out too, but in a much more restricted way. You may never consider travelling too far from your starting-point. People will have led you to expect very little and nobody will have taken you to a high hill and said, 'My son, one day all this will be yours.'

Whether you are rich or poor, though, there are great restrictions built into the map and your life may not change until you throw it away and rely on two things: your instinct about the right direction for you and your powers of observation.

Sooner or later, anyone who lives a rich life has learned to get lost and build their own map. What guides you in unfamiliar territory is not the map drawn up by somebody else for their own journey but the pictures in your head and heart and your own developing sense of what feels right. I notice this myself when I am navigating an unfamiliar place. As I move along, I am picking up all kinds of subliminal clues. I have an overall sense of the direction I am travelling in and whether I have veered too far off the path. I have an instinctive sense of where the light is falling and what time of day it is. I have flashbacks of other journeys that help me join up the dots, and when I pick up a familiar place name or a bus route I recognize my brain is busy building its own patterns. And if I go very wrong, well, that's all information too. It goes into the database for next time.

If you don't know what to do next or you've run out of ideas, try going out and getting lost. Take your worldly possessions in a red spotted handkerchief if you must, but it's more fun to rely on providence. Trust that your instinct will guide you home and know that you will experience your home differently. And have fun. Getting lost is a very creative act.

Too Soon to Tell

Forgive me if you've heard this story before but it's a good one to bear in mind whether you're on the thrilling or the daunting turn of the change cycle.

A poor man lived in a village with his son and a horse, and one day his horse ran away.

'Oh,' cried his neighbours, 'what a terrible calamity.'

'Maybe,' said the old man. 'Maybe not.'

One day his horse returned and with him came a magnificent herd of wild horses. The old man was able to corral them in his field.

'Oh,' cried the neighbours, 'what a wonderful piece of luck. Your fortune is made.'

'Maybe,' said the old man. 'Maybe not.'

His son began to break in the wild horses and one day he fell badly from one of them and broke his legs.

'Oh,' cried the neighbours, 'what an awful calamity.'

'Maybe,' said the old man. 'Maybe not.'

Before long a company of soldiers arrived in the village looking for conscripts for the army. They took all the young men away but they spared the old man's lame son.

'Oh,' wailed the villagers, 'how unfortunate we are. How very lucky you are.'

'Maybe,' said the predictable old man. 'Maybe not.'

And so it goes. As Mao Tse Tung is supposed to have said when he was asked what were the effects of the French Revolution, 'It's too soon to tell.'

There are no full stops in life, not even death. Yes, death is a full stop for us on this Earth and it may feel like the end of the world to those who have been bereaved. But bookshelves are full of stories of people who have not only survived crushing and annihilating tragedies but triumphed over them in the end. The most inspiring stories of all are about those people who lived through what should have destroyed them, from childhood cruelty to genocide, and turned their survival into inspiration for other people.

As Rudyard Kipling wrote in his perennially popular

poem *If*, triumph and disaster are both impostors. In the Middle Ages people used the metaphor of the wheel of fortune. People clung to the wheel and sometimes they were up, but just as surely they would circle down again. The wheel never stops turning.

If we engage with success and failure in our lives without seeing them as turns of the wheel, then we risk being destroyed by fear and grief or bloated by a sense of pride and invulnerability. People who get stuck in a sense of victimhood and failure self-destruct, but so do people who only identify with the trappings of victory. I only have to open my newspaper every morning to plot the downfall of famous people who have become so divorced from reality that they assume they have a God-given golden touch. They think can get away with arrogance, excess, cutting corners and abusing people, and they may, for a while, but the cost is high. Success is such a heady and isolating drug that it divorces its users from the simple truth that it can ebb away overnight. Nobody is invulnerable. We should all have, pinned to our mirrors, the words which a slave repeated to the Roman generals who rode in triumph through the streets: 'This also will pass.'

Is this good? Maybe. Is this terrible? Maybe. Maybe not. Whatever you are feeling, it will pass.

Change is continuous. That's all. It's not about us. So don't take it personally – not the intoxication of triumph, nor the black isolation of despair. Is my life a failure? It's too soon to tell.

If triumphalism and despair are both inappropriate responses to change, how should we react? With attention and with gratitude. I try to recognize each good moment of life as it passes. And as it passes I know that this is the nature of life. Thank you, thank you, thank you for all the good bits, for the sunny days, the gestures of love, the taste of pleasure, the spark of understanding. And thank you, even if I say it through gritted teeth, for the experiences of pain, failure and grief. These are where I find my humanity and understanding. These are where I learn compassion and empathy for others.

It is a gift to survive a self-managed disaster because if we stop wailing, 'Why me?' we can learn something. We can be on the way to wisdom. And we will have had experience that makes us both kinder and more useful to other people.

Is a life of change painful? Yes. Is a life of change exciting? Yes. Do I sometimes wish life would slow down and stand still? Often. Will it ever stand still? Never. Not in this life. Eternal rest is for the dead – or so we pray – but it is not for the living.

And is this life of constant change and adjustment worth living? Yes. Every single minute of it, as vividly and as consciously as possible, because this, also, will pass.

Mapping the New

I've moved house. My new home is only a mile away from my former home. I had lived in my former home for 12 years and, before that, I had lived in that district for 20 years. On a global scale I have hardly done more than turn over in my sleep. On a personal scale the little shift I made across the local map required as much internal mental effort as all the box-heaving and clothes-sorting and charity-shop giving it took to clear out my house and move in the first place.

The fact that I have brought some of my personal possessions with me, the fact that I know one or two people who live in the neighbouring streets and the fact that I used to live round the corner when I was in my early twenties give me the illusion that I have moved somewhere very familiar, but my brain is working overtime because nothing out there on the street matches its embedded internal systems. Emotionally, I am realizing that I have made a huge change.

Here are all the things that are different: I put my hand out to switch on the light and the light switch isn't there. The light comes into my bedroom from a different angle and wakes me at a different time. I am haunted by the uneasy feeling that nobody knows where I am. I don't know who my next-door neighbours are because I haven't seen them yet. My former friends, the ones I used to go walking with and meet for coffee, have disappeared over the rim of the Earth's curve. There is no point trying to meet them for the pre-breakfast walks on the common I used to enjoy because the rush-hour traffic flows between us like an impassable river. My post comes at a different time and I'm not getting the papers delivered, so my morning routine is different. I can't slope downstairs in a dressing gown to read the paper. I have to get dressed and go out and buy it.

Imperceptibly the whole city has shifted around me. Different buses rumble down the street and I walk a different way to get to a different station. The streets are lined with different shops and I am having to start from scratch to find out where to get my keys copied, my shoes mended, my clothes dry-cleaned and my eyes tested.

I find I am reacting to this mountain of micro-change in two different ways. At one level I am hugely excited. I wake every day with a holiday feeling because everything feels so different. I have escaped the everyday routine of years and each day brings new discoveries and treats. I've found the nearest park where I can walk. I've learned which café makes the best coffee. Walking round this new district on foot, I am discovering all kinds of interesting corners, gardens and architectural detail, historic plaques and unexpected alleys. I start each day with a sense of adventure.

On another level my brain blanks like a computer screen. I actually found myself sitting up in my new bed once and thinking, 'Well, this is very nice, but I think I'll go home now.' My intellect knew that this new place was home but all the rest of me, physical and emotional, suddenly longed for the old known world.

Change can be a lot to absorb. There are moments in each week when my mind simply can't take in another new piece of information, no matter how domestic and small. It is not as though I am learning the theory of relativity, but when even the location of the light switches has to be learned afresh I can't take anything for granted. Every new detail has to be checked, absorbed and stored, and the circuits get jammed. I find that in the midst of so much exciting newness I am longing for something familiar and boring. It would be a comfort to unravel my life and wake up in a place I could take for granted. Sometimes I switch from the excited holiday feeling to a state of tired depression.

Maybe I have made a huge mistake. Maybe I should have stayed where everybody knew my name.

This is my strategy: I am trying not to give in to a sense of panic when it rises. I am trying to be kind to my brain and give it little breaks.

To be honest, sometimes I just climb into my bed in my unfamiliar bedroom and seek the rebooting oblivion of sleep. If I am being a bit more conscious, I realize that meditation is the simplest thing I can do to clear my mind. So I just find an uncluttered spot in my new home, sit quietly, eyes closed, and return to the calm place within myself which is beyond change. I gently sweep out the incoming thoughts like leaves through an open door. I concentrate on my breathing until it becomes slow and steady and wait until I can feel myself becoming still.

My brain needs time and space in which to recreate itself and knit the new patterns on which survival depends. The irony is that once it knows where it is it may be time to move on.

Knowledge equals security equals boredom and the arrival of a kind of blindness and deafness. Discovery equals excitement, and constant alertness equals stress. Keeping the balance between stress and security, alertness and the sleep of familiarity is the work of a lifetime.

Risk Assessment

When you go to see a financial adviser one of the first things they ask you is what is your attitude to risk. Are you low risk? Do you want something safe where you will never lose your original investment but where you are unlikely to make high profits and may even find your investment eroded by inflation? Are you medium risk? Will you go for the chance of better profits with less protection for your investment? Or are you high risk? Would you prefer the chance of high profits even if your whole investment could collapse? Are you prepared to risk everything you've got in the hope of winning something much bigger?

Life's a gamble, of course, even when you are trying to do something as sensible as manage your money. Just because the stock market is fenced in with rules and regulations doesn't mean that it isn't like a large and elaborate poker game. Famous companies go broke. Advice you were given by solemn men in grey suits turns out to be worthless. Pensions you have saved up for years are suddenly undercut. In savings, as in the casino, it pays to spread your bets.

I am medium risk myself, in life as in my attitude to money. I love everything new – new fashions, new art, new friends, new music, new places, new ideas, new food. But I am also comfortable with and loyal to the old. I stick to family and friends. I draw strength from familiar places. And although I love the idea of adventure and have had a few, I'm scared of big risks. I haven't got the nerve to go paragliding or climb mountains or walk alone in wild places, though I wish I had. I do take risks, but most of those are the calculated kind.

It's helpful to understand your own attitude to risk when you contemplate a change, but your risk setting isn't fixed for life.

We've all had 'The hell with it!' moments, when we've thrown caution to the winds. I love the question 'Why not?' which often precedes a bit of self-indulgent or reckless behaviour. There are often plenty of reasons why not – it'll make you fat, broke or unhappy in the long term – but we must all have 'Why not?' moments just to feel alive.

Very risk-averse people may stay alive for longer, but are they really living?

We all know these people. They refuse to try unfamiliar food. They may never go abroad, but if they do they'll go to the same place again and again because they hate surprises. They buy the same clothes each season because they know what suits them and they don't want to stand out. They're suspicious of strangers and paint their walls a nice shade of magnolia. For the reward of avoiding all life's attempts to shock or surprise them, they pay the price of never being stretched or stimulated. They make fewer mistakes, but never know ecstasy.

High-risk people are exciting and bewildering to be around. They climb mountains, drive too fast, throw themselves into affairs with unsuitable people and try drugs because they have to experience everything first-hand. They crash sometimes and they don't get home in time for dinner, but they have a lot of fun, live on adrenaline and often create the innovative and original things in life. A lot of high-risk behaviour is fuelled by testosterone, which means it is more common among men, but there are some women on the high wire too, just fewer of them.

The emotions that go with risk make you feel alive. The emotions of excitement, intoxication, obsession, terror, relief and ecstasy hook gamblers of all kinds (especially the terror). High-risk people are adrenaline junkies, subsisting on the shots of fear that get their hearts and minds racing. I have a reckless friend who thinks that you should take a risk every day. A risk a day keeps boredom away. With it, you expand your boundaries. Without it, you descend slowly into the low-risk world of the comfortable and the comatose.

What is your attitude to risk? It's an important piece of self-knowledge which you can build into your decision-making. It is also something you can work on. Because I am a mildly risk-averse couch potato I once went on an Outward Bound-type course in the mountains where we abseiled and rock-climbed and gorge-walked. I did all of it, but I haven't done it again. It took me too far out of my comfort zone to be habit-forming.

I get the same kind of buzz from being involved with art. I fell in love with a picture beyond my means once and became obsessed. I told myself I had to walk away for 24 hours to see if the obsession would die down. It didn't, so I bought it, but I went through the same cycle of emotion with that picture – excitement and fear – that I had on the rock face. There wasn't the danger of falling, but another danger, that of wasting my money, which is a survival fear of a kind. They both make you lose sleep.

Risk-averse people really need to learn that the world can be a richer and more colourful place and that you feel dashing and daring if you step out of your rut once in a while. Sometimes I remember two teenage boys I once saw jumping from high rocks. 'Go on!' shouted one. 'Jump! It'll make you feel dead hard and cool.' It's fun to feel dead hard and cool. People like me tend to think too much about broken legs.

High-risk people have something that is invaluable, which is self-belief. Cautious people are afraid that things will go wrong. High-risk people always assume they will work out. Being a medium-risk person, I try to follow the Arabic proverb 'Trust in God and tether your camel.' I believe that God helps those who tether their camels.

Pathfinders

We go through life like nomads in the desert, hauling with us everything we think we'll need – tent, Primus stove, mosquito net – and lo, it turns out we have to climb mountains instead. Where are the climbing boots and snow-proof jackets, the crampons and the ice pick?

When you reach the edge of unknown territory it would be useful to have maps, but most of the people you ask only know the old ways. You have to make the new rules up for yourself, unless you can find a pathfinder.

Expectations are like that. I grew up with inherited ideas. I expected that marriage would last for life, that the perfect job existed, that I would have a middle age like my mother's and an old age like my grandparents'. I thought that my children would behave exactly as I had, and want the same life. I thought that I would retire at 60, though I'd never thought how I would do that and how I would pass the time. I hoped that at some magical point I would be handed the keys of the kingdom and live happily ever after. Some hope.

My ideas were completely out of date, not wanted on voyage. Nobody told me that life was going to be a constant process of reinvention. No one told me that life went down as well as up (though I should have guessed that from snakes and ladders). On second thoughts, maybe they did tell me and I didn't listen.

I still seem to spend part of each day re-evaluating, working out for myself how to have a fulfilled life and how to adjust when your children turn out to be different from you and how to build a social and an economic life when you are single, not married. And I've watched my parents and grandparents work a lot of things out for themselves because what they learned from their parents and grandparents didn't apply to them either, not in the details. Core values, the beliefs that lie at the heart of our actions, are longer-lasting, but re-evaluation is constant.

It's hard working everything out from first principles, so we naturally look for pathfinders. One pathfinder is never enough. You need a whole team and you need to cast your net wide. You may find them among your friends and family. There's always someone who's had sex before you, gone job-hunting before you, travelled in a country that interests you and can give you a clue to the territory. In particular we need pathfinders who are visionaries and rule breakers.

Our culture is full of pathfinders and you often stumble upon them unexpectedly. What they have to show you can come with the force of revelation. People who grow up in out-of-the-way places and manage to find their true path in life always talk, in interviews, about the revelation they had when they learned that someone else out there made music or designed clothes they loved or made a career out of chasing butterflies.

Somebody out there loves the same things that you do. Somebody out there is waiting to inspire and lead you by their example.

Even the mistakes of pathfinders can be inspiring. I always love to read about the French writer Colette. I don't think I would have liked her personally if I had met her, but she led the fullest of lives. She performed in the theatre and wrote wonderful books and libretti and plays and, being French, she also ran a beauty salon and ended up happily married to a much younger man who adored her. I find the richness and inclusiveness of her life inspiring.

To find your pathfinders, read, look and listen. You will come across them in fiction and cinema, in music and fashion, in science and politics. They could be dead or they could be living. When you do come across them they will hit you with the force of inspiration. You mean somebody like me could do something like that? Then it's not impossible…

Be prepared for one more thing. As your life changes, so will your pathfinders. The perfect role model for an energetic 20-year-old is not the pathfinder who will guide a mature woman into a rich and productive old age.

Be prepared for something else. If you are creative and

dogged enough you will look back and find that by forging your own path and finding your own direction you will have become a pathfinder for somebody else. The day that somebody told me that I was the woman they wanted to be was the day I thought I must be getting something right. You may want to be a doctor or a government minister or an Oscar winner, but few things make you feel quite as good as knowing that you have beaten a path for others to follow.

Stepping Stones

I have made my way through life on stepping stones. This isn't the only way. Look around and you will see that people build their lives very differently. Some hack their way through the jungle, slashing and burning and transforming the landscape. Some are always taking wild leaps into the dark. Sometimes they land on their feet. Sometimes they miss and fall. Some people are so paralysed by the risks inherent in change that they crouch in the undergrowth for years, becoming more entrenched as time passes them by. Some are full of wild schemes that they never try out. Some waste years longing to be rescued. When it comes to making changes in life I have found that stepping stones work for me.

Using stepping stones as your method of forward motion means that you never make a leap without having a landing place. It may not be dry land. It may not be a settled resting-place, but it will be movement in the direction in which you wish to travel.

What do stepping stones look like? A stepping stone towards the change you really want will not be the change in its entirety. So if it's a dream job you are after it won't be the dream job, but neither will the stone you are leaving behind. Stepping stones are the stages that will get you there when the distance between where you stand and where you want to be is too great to cross in one leap.

You create stepping stones by doing research and making connections. Say you are after that dream job. You can't get it straightaway, so you consider training and voluntary work. You offer to do unpaid work if it will get you nearer your goal. You read articles that name people who do the kind of work you want or who could help you, and you write to these people, asking for their advice and if you could maybe even meet them. They can only say 'no' or, more usually, not reply at all. But one 'yes' could make all the difference.

Even moving via stepping stones means taking risks – the risk of putting your ideas out into the open and looking foolish – but you must do that if you are to make change.

So you start moving in your chosen direction, stepping stone by stepping stone. If you want to make films, you get a camera and start making something you can show to other people. If you want to write, you start writing and join a writing group. If you want to make political change, you go to meetings and demonstrations and join lobby groups. You volunteer. You meet like-minded people and one thing leads to another.

Stepping stones are not just about finding a new job. They can be moves towards the kind of life you really want to live.

Have you thought of moving abroad? Go on holiday to another country and do a recce. Do you feel you've outgrown your friends? Get involved with an activity that attracts you and you will meet like-minded people. Do you long to move to a different part of town? Stop fantasizing about it and start walking round new neighbourhoods. Consider renting while you look. Life doesn't have to be all or nothing with no safety net. It can be trial and error.

Making your way on stepping stones means building on the great truth that one thing leads to another. And one person leads to another. When you make your intention known to the people you meet in the gym or in your terrible job or at your local party meeting, somebody may say that their friend's aunt or their neighbour's cousin knows somebody who knows something about what you want. Always follow up leads. Every lead is a stepping stone. And one stone leads to another.

If you have ever tried to cross a stream by creating your own stepping stone you will know that it can be a hit or miss business. The stone you are trying to position ahead of yourself disappears under the water. Or it is insecure and wobbles wildly when you try to step on it. This doesn't matter. Cast about for more stones and just keep chucking them into the water. Sooner or later you will create a firm footing.

The other crucial point about stepping stones is that you never step off the one you are on until the next one is in place and will take your weight. I once made the mistake of giving up one job before I had secured the next. You recover, of course, but you have made life harder for yourself. Waist-deep in flowing water is not an easy base from which to make a change. Even the smallest stone, the least promising job, the least likely contact, is a springboard to the next.

One day you will step onto a stone which leads to dry land. Congratulations. You've made it across. All those letters and e-mails, all those contacts, all that research, all that unpaid preparation, lobbying and persistence have carried you through to the place where you wanted to be.

Do you still want to be there? Or has your mind leaped ahead to a new destination across another wide stretch of water? It doesn't matter now because you've learned the art of getting there. Stepping stones will get you anywhere you want to go.

May You Live in
Interesting Times

When you are young and life seems slow and boring and you moan that nothing ever changes around here, you long for excitement and revolution. The first time you hear the Chinese curse 'May you live in interesting times,' you can't understand why that would be a curse. What could be more fun?

In the spring of 1978 I was living in Afghanistan with my husband and our six-month-old daughter. It was a great time to be there. The country was peaceful, ancient and extremely beautiful. Our windows looked out over rows of poplar trees to the snow-capped mountains that surrounded Kabul. During the week my husband worked as a doctor for Save the Children, training Afghan doctors and nurses in rural health care. On Thursday afternoons we left our modern house on the edge of the city and drove round the feet of the mountains and their encrustations of flat-topped houses to do our shopping in the bazaars.

I loved the bazaars of Kabul. In a warren of narrow streets and alleyways you could change money, examine carpets, get clothes made to measure, buy melons, huge pomegranates and delicious grapes, try on heavy silver necklaces and find pots and pans. There was a timelessness to the activity of the bazaars, even when there were anachronistic details like the calculators of the cross-legged money-changers or the red jewel that turned out to be a chunk of reflector from a car light.

On the afternoon of 25 April my husband arrived home and announced that the presidential palace was surrounded by tanks. Nobody knew why. At the end of our side street we found that there were tanks in the main road too. There were also buses and bicycles and taxis and horses and carts and plenty of people on foot. Life appeared to be normal, given a tank or two, so we drove on.

It was very quiet as we did our shopping and something made us decide to head home early. As we drove through the streets there was a series of sudden explosions close by and the Land Rover seemed to leap into the air. Home suddenly seemed very far away.

During our anxious drive through an increasingly empty city, past roadblocks that had sprung up, we saw that a pair of jet fighters had appeared in the skies and seemed to be circling overhead.

Back home we locked our garden gate carefully and set about our normal routine of unpacking our shopping, preparing supper and bathing the baby. At one point we stood, damp baby in arms, staring out of the back window of our house towards the city centre, through the V-shape of the mountains, while the jets spectacularly divebombed the area of the presidential palace. In the meantime the long avenue off which we lived was preparing to be the scene of an all-night tank battle.

Nothing can be more interesting than finding yourself caught in a fast-moving moment of change, be it war, crime or natural disaster. It's terrifying maybe, baffling possibly, but interesting absolutely. That night in Kabul when the history of the country shifted on its axis was one of the most interesting nights of my life. At first we phoned friends in other parts of town to find out what was going on and nobody knew. My husband even thought of going off for his regular game of squash until he phoned his squash partner and was told that he was sheltering from shelling under his kitchen table. Then the phone lines went dead. Whatever was happening, we were on our own.

And it went on being interesting. We could hear the

sounds of shelling, bombing and machine-gun fire. I sat writing an over-excited letter home to my parents, not knowing when they would get it. The journalist in me was thrilled even though – maybe because – I knew we were in a dangerous situation.

Excitement and fear are inseparable companions. They are both fuelled by large amounts of adrenaline. The mind races. The body is alert. Excitement is pleasurable because you feel so alive. In Afghanistan, as a journalist I knew that I was living in the middle of the biggest story of my life and yet, as is often the way when you are in the very middle of fast-changing events, I didn't have the slightest clue what was going on around me. Then, even as I was writing my letter home, an explosion went off so close to the house that the plate-glass windows rattled. My husband and I leaped straight up the stairs, grabbed our sleeping baby from her cot and ran back down to the kitchen, where we barricaded ourselves in with mattresses and tuned into the BBC World Service to hear if somebody out there could tell us what was happening to Afghanistan. That was how we passed the night.

As day dawned the machine-gun fire, shelling and bombing stopped. Everything went quiet. The baby woke up, peered over the edge of her carry-cot to see her parents lying on the kitchen floor and crowed with delight. Something made me decide to hard boil all the eggs in case the electricity was cut.

Gradually our neighbours emerged from hiding with their own stories of the night. One family had been lined up against the wall by gunmen and had had to talk themselves out of being shot. Another neighbour had been blown off his feet by a shell which had come through the window of his house. He and his family had spent the night in the garden and found dead bodies on the doorstep in the morning.

We began to go out onto the streets and found bullet-marked walls and broken glass everywhere. And still nobody had an explanation for what had happened.

In time we learned that there had been a Russian-backed coup d'état and the President and all his family had been shot. Within weeks Russian advisers had moved into the ministries and the many Western aid schemes had become paralysed. By the end of that year the new American ambassador had been shot in a botched kidnap rescue attempt and most Westerners, including us, had left the country. A year later the Red Army rumbled in, to be followed, in due course, by the growth of the Northern Alliance, the rise of the Taliban, Al Quaida and the American-led bombing of the country.

Interesting times are interesting because they are always times of change. You have to pay extreme attention to understand what is going on. What is at stake is the way things are and the way they are going to be. The status quo, whether of a country or a marriage or a way of thinking, is shifting fast. You can't afford to fall asleep.

The Chinese are right, though. Interesting times are far too unsettling to live in. Even if your life is not at stake, your way of life might be. And who can be alert all the time? We all deserve space in which we can rest, even if we are only preparing for the next attack of interestingness.

I offer a blessing instead of a curse. May you survive interesting times and live to enjoy a little restful boredom.

Brainfreeze

Change is good but too much change, too fast, is over-whelming. When the brain has to take in too many new ideas at once it freezes and keeps replaying the same scene. In a highly dangerous situation this is a symptom of post-traumatic stress syndrome.

I was in a café once when there was a violent argument over drugs and a man suddenly pulled a gun and put it to an innocent bystander's head. A shot was fired into the ceiling, there was a scuffle and the man ran. Nobody was hurt, but several people, including me, were shocked and traumatized. I couldn't think of anything else for hours. Days later, when I saw a man suddenly raise his arm in a street to point out the way, I flinched. I thought he held a gun. I was still suffering from brainfreeze.

The mind gets stuck on the good stuff too. When I was house-hunting I knew I'd found somewhere I liked because my mind moved right into the new space. One day I had room in my mind for a lot of different ordinary things. The next day I was completely stuck in a groove, hanging curtains at my possibly new windows, arranging furniture in my possibly new home, digging up my possibly new garden, painting new colours on my possibly new walls. And I did all of this before I even knew the place was mine.

I don't have to tell you how obsessed the mind becomes when we meet somebody to whom we are attracted. The new person, the whole new life they represent, turn into occupying forces which deflect the brain from all its habitual courses. Love is a very bad case of brainfreeze.

What is the answer to an attack of brainfreeze? The first is to recognize that you have it. But maybe we don't need an answer. Maybe it is fine to be magnetized into a state of preoccupied trance. Sometimes it can be very pleasant indeed. I love the state of reverie. Do you know that poem by Emily Dickinson?

> *To make a prairie, all it takes is clover and one bee, and reverie.*
> *And reverie alone will do, if bees are few.*

Reverie alone will do to make a plant into a prairie, a glance into a love affair, a five-minute viewing into a new dream home.

But the other kind of brainfreeze is not pleasant at all. It can be highly destructive. When brainfreeze meets rage and a sense of injury it can become obsession. Rejected lovers with brainfreeze turn into stalkers. Sacked workers with brainfreeze turn into disappointed people who turn their energies into nursing an injury when it would be far healthier for them to dust themselves down, pick up what's left of their self-respect and move on.

Do you know the story of Greyfriars Bobby? He was a Scottish dog with a very bad case of brainfreeze. His master died and the dog refused to move from his graveside. This is a touching story of loyalty and you will find a little statue to Greyfriars Bobby in the Edinburgh graveyard where he spent years of his life. But too many people turn into Greyfriars Bobbies. When life changes we must adapt or die. Or turn into little statues mourning for a past which will never return. I'd rather be a sentient human being with all the pain and confusion that entails than a monument to brainfreeze.

With brainfreeze, the brain is behaving very like an over-loaded computer and some of the same remedies work. One of the first things you are told when your computer freezes or starts behaving oddly is simply to switch the thing off. The idea is that a miraculous process might then soothe the traumatized computer and allow it to put itself back together in the right order. The same thing can happen with brains if you give them a chance.

An overloaded brain needs to take itself somewhere very

quiet and go as blank as possible. There is room in your brain for all sorts of new and shocking ideas, but not all at once. An emergency solution, in pressing circumstances, could simply be to leave the room and lock yourself in the loo while you calm down. It helps to take long slow breaths. For non-emergencies, when you have a bigger time-scale to play with, the principle is still the same. You need to switch off and allow your brain to adjust its settings. You need to take a break from the onslaught of stimulus.

So, when you recognize that you have a case of brainfreeze, it is time to retreat and regroup. Take time out in the form that works best for you. If your thinking is really obsessive, it can be very hard to switch off. You need to replace your repetitive ideas with something more urgent, preferably something physical. When you have to concentrate in order not to fall off a horse or capsize a boat or even mess up a new dance step then you are giving your frozen brain a very necessary rest. And a rested brain is ready to cope with the next change.

The Power of the People

There are two great delusions about changing the world. One is that you are a martyr because you have to do everything on your own. The other is that you are a hero because you have to do everything on your own. The first one gets more of a grip as you get older and gloomier. The second one is a fantasy of youth and is much more fun.

Who hasn't dreamed about being a superhero who single-handedly saves the world? Ours is the struggle, true, but ours are the glory and the adulation, which, of course, we shrug off modestly before going back to our humble ways. Harry Potter, Frodo, Superman, Pippi Longstocking, Wonder Woman – the saviour has many names and many shapes. Why not us? It could happen. People and animals and supernatural beings could appear to give us a helping hand, but in the darkest hours we could be the ones who single-handedly face down the forces of evil.

All this gets a bit tiring as you pass adolescence. It turns out that we don't have the power to save the world single-handedly and, worse, it takes all the power we have just to get to work on time or get our children to do their homework. We may worry about pollution and the war on terror, but there's not much energy over at the end of the day to do much about it. It turns out we aren't Superman or Superwoman after all. And if we're not careful, we find ourselves turning to the martyr fantasy and groaning under the burden of having to do everything on our own. Only we don't.

Solitary struggle is a bit of an indulgence. Whatever it is you are trying to do, there are people out there who can help lighten the load, spread the message, rally the troops and save the world. Every movement, whether in politics or art or philosophy, began with a handful of people who found they thought the same way. Every difficult human situation, whether it is solitary confinement, caring for the elderly, mental illness or single parenthood, has attracted support organizations and campaigners, pathfinders who have been there before and helpers who will give encouragement.

When it comes to changing the world in a big way, there is so much more momentum in a movement than in a single human being. I don't know what you care about, but I am sure you care about something. It might be arresting the pace of climate change. It might be global justice. It might be workers' rights or regeneration through art. It might be conserving threatened buildings or rerouting roads or challenging the dominance of supermarkets. Whatever it is, I promise you that, no matter where you live, there are other people who think and feel as you do.

When you find those people you will be so much more effective and your life will be much richer. Where do you find them?

Everywhere. You find them through your passions. You find them through the internet, through political organizations, in centres of education and learning, in pressure groups and charities, on evening classes and courses, in the pages of publications that report on the topics that interest you most. You meet them at your children's school gate or among your neighbours when you start a petition.

The benefits of bonding with other people come at every level and I wouldn't place political action above the life-enhancing plus of friendship. I know what it is to feel lonely and isolated and excluded, but when I challenge myself on it I admit that this is an illusion which I can dispel just as soon as I walk onto the street or pick up the phone. Solitude is valuable, but we evolved to be social and joining in doesn't just prolong our life (which it does), it makes it worth living.

My Samurai Partner

Marianna is my Samurai partner. A Samurai partner is a friend, but more than a friend. It is a friend with rules and parameters attached, and when you are contemplating change in your life or struggling with change that is happening to you, a Samurai partner is a very precious thing.

I can't remember exactly how Marianna and I fell into this relationship, but we were already friends and we had ambitions and organized minds and Marianna had once gone on a course called Samurai which involved getting up at dawn and changing your life. Part of the Samurai strategy was to have a buddy to meet up with regularly so you could keep each other on track. I don't know what happened to Marianna's previous Samurai partner, but I became her new one. At a tumultuous time in both our lives when we were full of dreams and obstacles to those dreams, we would meet, notebooks and pens in hand, and we would analyse and we would envision and we would plan.

The essence of a Samurai partnership is equal listening. It's not like an everyday friendship where two people will get together over a drink or a coffee. Then one will let off steam and the other will nod and grunt and, as soon as there is a gap in the conversation, will throw in their two penn'orth of gratuitous advice or, more likely, say, 'That's exactly like this thing that's happened to me,' and go off on a rant of their own while friend number one waits patiently for the chance to bring the conversation round their way again. Of course this kind of friendship is therapeutic and vital, but a Samurai partnership isn't like that. Samurai partnerships get things done.

At the beginning of a Samurai session you both decide how long you want to speak for, and when you have decided whether you want 15 minutes or half an hour or an hour each, you decide who goes first. The role of the listening partner is to be wholly attentive to the one who talks. This is not the time for personal experiences of your own – that can come later. Your job is to pay extreme attention, ask elucidating questions, maybe make notes. You may spot inconsistencies and have useful suggestions. Your aim is to help the other person arrive at a plan of action, preferably one to be executed in manageable stages and within a realistic time frame, all of which you write down. When the allotted time is up, you stop. You can always return to tidy up the loose ends once the second person has taken their turn at talking through their situation.

As I remember it, when Marianna and I first started working together she was thinking of going to live abroad and my marriage was falling apart. We came at our problems from all kinds of angles. We spent time drawing up a five-year plan and a two-year plan that covered all areas of our lives. By the time we left each session we had an action list to be carried out before we met again in a week's or two weeks' time.

The basis of this relationship was trust and somehow that the two of us were on the same wavelength at the time. We were also both energetic and efficient. We both had blank spots which were easier for the other one to see. I think we also genuinely wanted the best for each other. We wanted to see each other fulfilled and happy.

That was 15 years ago now. Marianna went off to live in Greece and we haven't had a Samurai session in years, but I valued them and I still value her friendship and I would recommend a Samurai relationship to anybody. Life coaches charge an awful lot of money, though they are disinterested and they have professional skills of their own to apply. But if you are not in complete confusion and if you are genuinely committed to making changes and you find a like-minded buddy, team up. It can be a special relationship. I have a number of good friends I confide in, but only one Samurai partner.

People, Not Projects

Can you change another person? The history of the world revolves around that question. The happiness of communities, of families, couples and individuals revolves around that question. And your happiness revolves around it too, since nobody seems to get through life without being the target of somebody else's attempt to change them or being seized with the idea that it would be a great idea to change somebody else.

My advice, like Mr Punch's advice to those about to get married, is: *Don't*. Life has taught me that attempts to change other people are infuriating for the changee and frustrating for the would-be changer. What is the message given by the changer? 'You're just not good enough the way you are.' What is the message ultimately given by the changee? 'Back off and leave me alone. If you don't like me the way I am you know what you can do.'

So why do we do it? And when we do it, why do we do it in such demeaning and unsuccessful ways?

I think we do it for two reasons. One is that we are simply used to having it done to us from early childhood and the other is that nobody is perfect.

The very process of growing up is the process of being trained to fit in. Parents, families and schools apply constant pressure to teach us manners, tribal customs and acceptable habits. The first explosion of resentment against other people telling us what to do occurs around two years old, when we first take on board the enormity of the 'no' word and start to scream it right back. Feel sorry for the two-year-old. With none of the advantages of size, age, authority or power, it is standing alone against the might of the universe and the only weapon it has is the tantrum. The tantrum is quite a good weapon – it gets you noticed – and in some cases it will work, but mostly size, age, authority and power will have the last word and the two-year-old will be on the way to being socialized.

It is because most adults have learned to be reasonable and not to throw tantrums when crossed that one half of us thinks it is worth trying to improve the other half – we know we (probably) won't be screamed at. Another reason we think it is worth trying is that we have learned that all human beings are a work in progress and it is a lot easier to spot what needs doing to someone else than to focus on ourselves.

I think men and women are equally guilty of this. For every woman trying to improve her man (and they are legion), there is a Svengali or a Professor Higgins who likes the idea of manipulating and moulding a woman. We are all a great makeover opportunity for somebody, and as soon as we get close to another person the corners where we don't fit cry out to be planed and polished.

We would all save ourselves a lot of pain if we learned to take the whole person on board at the very beginning. So much information is given to us from the start which we choose to ignore. Try to separate someone's essential nature, their truthfulness, intelligence and reliability from their acquired manners and charm. Note how they treat other people as well as you. Look out for danger signs like bad temper. And beware of the urge to rescue damaged and difficult people – they can drag you down. If you realize that you are constantly drawn to abusive people, try to pull back and examine your own behaviour.

Reading other people goes hand in hand with self-knowledge. How many times have you watched friends falling for people you know will make them unhappy in the long run? Be your own friend and treat your happiness like a favourite child. Know what makes it thrive and what threatens it. Protect it and don't give it as a hostage to somebody who might harm it. When you meet someone new, be aware if your friends are not quite as enamoured as you are. Their sight might be clearer than yours.

Of course people can change. Of course people can be redeemed by love. Of course people can flower and grow with the right person by their side, but that is usually because they decide to reclaim themselves. It can't be done by force. You might be a good influence, but I think personal change happens as a result of strength, clear boundaries and love. I don't think it ever happens as a result of coercion, criticism and nagging.

And life has taught me that if you can't change the other person or change yourself, then you may have to tackle the same lessons in a different relationship.

Good Times, Bad Times

When I was 40 years old I had a jolly birthday party. My friends came and the sun shone. We drank pink champagne in the garden and ate strawberries. My children looked delicious. My husband was charming. I drank champagne and looked at my friends and felt happy and I took silent, very satisfying stock of my life.

Forty felt pretty good. I loved my husband and we were getting on well together. My children were adorable. We had a house with a strange wild garden and, although it was part of the city, I woke up each morning to the sound of birdsong. I was really enjoying my job. I'd been given a diary column to write which involved getting out and meeting people and that was fun. I couldn't see that life could be any better.

Of course everything changed. The earth was shrinking under that house with the lovely garden and cracks were beginning to open up in the foundations and make their way up the walls.

There were cracks in the foundations of my life too, though I didn't know it.

Before I was 45 years old the job, husband and house had all gone. My children were all that was left. And I was still there, of course. I hadn't sought change, but change had sought me and I had to adapt or die.

I don't know how my life would have turned out if everything had stayed the same after that moment of contentment and self-congratulation. It is unimaginable, because too many things would have had to have been different. My house would have had to have been built on solid ground with no big trees near it, but then we'd bought it because we loved the trees and the birds that sang in their branches even as their roots were undermining our foundations. My husband would have had to have been happy working long hours at the hospital and coming home to the suburbs every night, but he wasn't, and actually, I'd married him because I'd loved his spirit of adventure, his energy and his longing to travel and explore. It was me that changed, not him.

As for the job, I wasn't that sorry when the editor decided that diary writing wasn't really my strength. He was right. He sent me back to write my column, but I'm not good at going backwards. I had that feeling of *déjà vu* which is death to enthusiasm at work. It was time for me to make a change myself. I uprooted and moved to another paper where I was much happier.

That period was one of the major railway junctions of my life. I crossed tracks without knowing what the final destination was going to be. I still don't know. I certainly hadn't got the Happy Ever After I thought I'd read on the departure board.

There were other things I'd read wrongly too. I'd ignored,

literally, the cracks in the wall. I'd married a man because he was adventurous and grown unhappy because he wasn't stable and predictable. There was writing on the wall which I'd ignored in my marriage as well as in my house.

But when I look back there must have been good fairies at that birthday party, because the shell of the old life falling away revealed whole new worlds for me to explore. I remember the very worst times came with some very good times. I remember one day, nearly five years later, on which my life seemed to pivot. I'd lost a marriage and joined a symphony chorus. We were recording Leonard Bernstein's *Candide* with Leonard Bernstein conducting, and I was so bowled over by the experience that I'd devoted my weekly newspaper column to what that was like. On the day the column came out my personal life was at its lowest ebb, but we were recording with Bernstein and the London Symphony Orchestra in the famous Abbey Road studios that night. I left my children with friends and turned up at the studios, thrilled to be there. Over 200 people – orchestra, soloists, chorus, conductor – filled the studio and someone had shown Leonard Bernstein my column because, in front of those 200 people, he called out my name and then told me I was brilliant. At the end of the session he embraced me and I floated home to my children in a cloud of euphoria and told them I wasn't going to wash for a week.

Nobody but me knew that I was having the worst week of my life and now it was the best as well. 'Joy and woe are woven fine,' we sang as the chorus in *Candide*. 'Life is neither good nor bad. Life is life and all we know.'

My life didn't magically change that night. It went on being bad. And good. And good and bad. And so it goes. But it did go better, because whatever changes makes room for something new.

Always and Never

As I celebrated my fortieth birthday, I was given a new map of the future, one that gave me hope and comfort. Some friends gave me a visit to an astrologer as a birthday present. The astrologer looked at my birth chart and told me cheerfully that I was born for change. She told me that a clear message from my chart was that for the whole of the rest of my life I would be doing new things.

My relief was immediate and huge. I'd been finding the search for stability very hard work, but I couldn't see another way to be. I'm a Gemini and full of curiosity, but I'd been brought up by a generation which longed, through Depression and world war, for stability. Divorce was rare in my parents' generation, even though people became widows and orphans. And jobs were for life, if you could get them. I was always told that employers would never take you seriously if you kept moving around.

This wasn't how I felt. I liked novelty and movement. I hated the feeling of being stuck. I was always stimulated by new ideas and experiences. I loved change and got bored easily, but my upbringing made me feel guilty about it. And now here was this complete stranger, knowing nothing about me but with a map of the night sky before her, telling me that change was going to be my life's companion.

What she didn't say was that change can be painful as well as exciting, involuntary as well as sought-after. And change can also be very slow, slower than you want it to be. It took years for my marriage to unravel. And it took years for the agonizing process of inspection and monitoring and arguments with insurance companies that accompanied the cracks in my walls. My fizzing happiness on my fortieth birthday was followed by some very difficult years.

But I look back and I can see, with hindsight, that I received helpful messages and guidance. When the astrologer told me that I would always be doing something new I interpreted this as fun, which was just as well. It didn't occur to me, in the temporary fortress of a happy life, that change is often difficult and devastating and that some of the new things I was going to be doing might not be fun at all.

There is a constant tension in life between the idea of 'always' and the idea of 'never'. When we are in a good bit we usually say, 'Why can't life always be like this?' When we are in a bad bit we often say, 'I never want to have to go through this again.' There is a tendency, when life is hard, to think we will never be happy again. We are much better off without the hammer blows of 'always' and 'never'.

But when the astrologer said 'always changing', she turned the full stop into a dance. Her 'always' gave me comfort because it implied survival and a kind of constant returning to balance.

When I am in danger of seeing my life as a full stop I remember that change is a friend. Change is guaranteed. It's the art of returning to balance that takes a lifetime to learn. Sometimes we focus on the change and sometimes we focus on the 'always', but they are both there, if we look. And the most comfortable viewpoint is somewhere between the two.

Beautiful Upheaval

For three glorious years I had a job which got me a ticket to the Paris collections. I loved everything about it. I loved waking up in my Paris hotel room and tripping over the Pont Royal each morning to the courtyards of the Louvre where the shows took place. I loved seeing what fashion journalists from round the world wear (mostly black). I adored the shows themselves – the theatricality, the inventiveness, the creative leaps of imagination. I learned that a beautiful woman in a pitch-perfect dress made by a designer and a team at the peak of their mastery and skill can move you to tears like a mountain landscape or a field of daffodils. I learned that wit and the cross-fertilization of ideas expressed in clothes can be as mentally stimulating as reading a great book or listening to new music. I learned to respect fashion at this level as a manifestation of art.

What we all hungered for as we trampled each other to

find a seat and waited, tired and hungry, for hours for shows to begin late, was something new. The silent bubbles above our heads read, 'Surprise me. Shock me. Excite me. Please me.' A good show filled us with elation. If a show was dull, we sighed and left feeling as bored and depressed as if we were mourning the emptiness of our own wardrobes.

Fashion is the supreme example of change for change's sake. It elevates planned obsolescence to an art form. As the legendary editor of American *Vogue*, Anna Wintour, wrote, 'Fashion's ceaseless allure lies in its promise of beautiful upheaval, twice yearly.'

She also wrote, 'As we know from even the most benign transitions in our own lives, change is always disturbing.' But change is also addictive and the eternal yearning for new looks, new ideas and new clothes which begins with the universal words 'I've got nothing to wear' is our homage to the power of the new.

If you are wearing a puritanical hat, this restless craving for novelty is the work of the Devil. One of the fundamental laws of any kind of hierarchical organization, be it educational, military or spiritual, is to create a uniform. This lifts the individual out of vanity, certainly, but also out of this perpetual quicksilver distracting craving for transformation and novelty. It's true that the love of the new is temptation in its most reprehensible and frivolous form. It is also the most accessible and everyday manifestation of human creativity and the universal impulse to decorate and beautify. I don't see anything wrong with that.

What I learned at the Paris collections is that if you take

something we all have to do every day, which is to get dressed, and apply the highest standards of creative rigour and craftsmanship to it, then you will produce an art form. Just because the works of art hang on the human body instead of a wall doesn't diminish their creative force.

And I also realize that this constantly changing art form has its roots in a natural cycle of change, one that affects everything we do: the change in the seasons. It is not an accident that high fashion in its most refined form comes from countries which are subject to the clear demarcation of summer, winter, autumn and spring. Changing seasons of sun and rain, heat and cold, autumn winds and summer heatwaves require a lot of clothes. In a climate like the one that I was born into, you can experience these rapid changes in a single day and thus the idea of dressing in layers was born, with an umbrella added for safety. If you live in the tropics, the same length of cloth will do all year round, and indeed for most of your life. That won't work in New York, Paris or London.

In Ethiopia, the national dress for men and women is white cotton robes turning to grey and ageing to brown before they disintegrate. The longer I lived there, despite the extraordinary natural beauty of the country, the more I craved the stimulation of colour and fashion. I got my mother to airmail me a copy of *Vogue* and it was like a draught of clear water in a desert. It satisfied my senses, but it also elevated my spirit. I pored over that one copy for a whole year, luxuriating in every detail in every photograph. I sucked the juice out of it. It taught me that in this life, certainly if you are a woman, the need for the beautiful upheaval of a change of style is not a whim but a fundamental thirst. We may have difficulty with change, but we were born to change clothes.

Made in Error

I will never forget my first art lesson. I can see myself, at five years old, seated in front of a huge piece of paper with a brush in my hand and some unbearably exciting glass jars full of thick coloured paint on the desk before me. A teacher stood at the front of the class and she told us that we were going to make patterns. Patterns! I couldn't wait to begin. I plunged my brush into the glass jar of paint and made a lovely big square on the paper.

I don't remember what the teacher did next exactly, but I remember the paralysing shame. I had done something wrong. I had started before everyone else. I had started before she had explained what we were meant to do. I had made a big stand-out mistake and it was staring up at me from the middle of my spoiled paper. If a five-year-old can get any smaller, that is what I got.

If only somebody – preferably the teacher – had told me

that it was OK to make mistakes. If only she had told me, when I was young enough to incorporate it into my life and play with the idea, that mistakes and unexpected changes happen to everyone. If only she had told me that life was simply crammed full of trial and error, mistakes and spoilings, choppings and changings, and the only thing that really mattered was how quickly and how creatively you could recover from them. If only she'd told me that the path of invention and science and art was littered with mistakes that turned out to be revelations and that human progress depended on them. But she didn't tell me anything like that. She just told me I was wrong.

I can remember exactly what my picture looked like to this day and how it was different from everyone else's. We were supposed to do repeating patterns, so I doggedly got on with making a repeating pattern and there was my inappropriate coloured square in the middle of rows of unadventurous and apologetic loops. As my mum said afterwards, it looked like a large crowd of people carrying a single flag.

Incidents like these can cut our creativity off at the roots and leave us afraid of making mistakes for the rest of our lives. Nobody tells us that Winston Churchill once defined leadership as 'going from failure to failure without losing enthusiasm'. Nobody tells us that the playwright Samuel Beckett urged people to 'Fail again. Fail better.' If they had, then we would have had an education in the art of taking things in our stride and encouragement in escaping the deadening idea of perfection.

The fact is, once you understand how creativity really works, you understand that there is no such thing as a mistake. Mistakes are better seen as errors, wanderings from the path, and truly creative people deal with these wanderings by incorporating them, using them as departure-points and fresh stimuli to new possibilities. That teacher could have rescued me from shame and turned me round by showing me how I could incorporate my bold square into the patterns she wanted us to explore.

In the arts, error is encouraged. Actors go to improvisation class not only in order to loosen up their own creativity but also because things go wrong in live performance and you have to be free and spontaneous enough to keep going. It's no use Juliet freezing to the spot when Romeo forgets to feed her the right Line. You might even have to improvise on Shakespeare.

Visual artists go wrong on purpose. I wish I'd known that when I was five. I wish I'd known that the Surrealists, in particular, devised all kinds of methods to bring the unexpected and unpredictable into their work. They wanted to lose control, not keep it.

I once went on a course run by Tate Modern on the art of mistakes and we were challenged to go away and create systems that would bring randomness and error into our own work. They could be anything from picking random words out of the dictionary to incorporate into a poem to cutting up a painting and rearranging it as collage. I heard of a woman who accidentally walked into a plate-glass window and used her accident as a basis for art, and another woman who turned her cancer X-rays into paintings.

Of course sometimes an error is a catastrophic change. It's hard to see how a surgeon can make a creative turnaround when he's taken out the wrong kidney, but using your cancer X-rays as a basis for paintings is a very powerful example of triumphing over disaster. As the writer Paul Virilio said, when he curated an exhibition devoted to accidents, 'Daily life is becoming a kaleidoscope of incidents and accidents, catastrophes and cataclysms in which we are endlessly running up against the unexpected.'

You can be sure that accidents will happen. That isn't important. What really matters is how we use them to keep going.

When unexpected change happens, a lifetime's experience of teachers and parents prompts you to say, 'Oh no!' But catch yourself out. Try saying, 'That's interesting,' instead. Or better still, 'What a fantastic piece of luck.'

Freefall and the Cliff Edge

There comes a point in the experience of change when you have to let go of the trapeze and launch yourself into the air. This is the moment of commitment. All the moments leading up to it may be moments of doubt, of fear, of paralysing indecision and stomach-lurching panic, but the moment of launching yourself into the air is the moment of no turning back.

It can be surprisingly peaceful. It can be a release. All sorts of new discoveries can grow from it that couldn't have occurred to you until the commitment was made. Robyn Davidson, who crossed the Australian desert single-handed with camels, said that the only difficult moment was deciding that she was going to do it. After that, the challenges and privations and physical danger were simply things to take into her stride.

When I was at school we studied Shakespeare's *King Lear*

and one scene always stayed in my mind. The blind Gloucester is being led by Edgar, who persuades him that they are standing on the brink of a terrible cliff:

> *Come on, sir; here's the place: stand still.*
> *How fearful and dizzy 'tis, to cast one's eyes so low!*
> *The crows and choughs that wing the midway air*
> *Show scarce so gross as beetles.*

The despairing Gloucester jumps, thinking he will fall to his death, but he only lands on the grass. Still, Edgar persuades him that he has fallen and survived. His life is a miracle.

I've always loved that scene, with its vertiginous poetry as a metaphor of change and a poetic encapsulation of what fear does to a perturbed mind. How often in life have I metaphorically paced along the edge of some cliff, only to find, when I stepped forward, that I didn't fall but landed easily on solid ground. The cliff edge is usually farther off than you think. The projected fall may only be a step.

In the year before I wrote this book I lurched from cliff edge to cliff edge and once or twice I fell and even then it didn't feel like the fall from a rockface. Somehow I was still able to step forward on solid ground. Here is my year. Both parents ill, mother recovers, father dies. My father's death was less painful than the weeks of cliff-edge walking that preceded it. When death came it was a low reverberating blow that stunned me into a kind of invisible psychic shutdown, but it was also a release from the terrible tension of anxiety, fear and pity and the physical exhaustion of keeping watch.

No sooner was the funeral over than a buyer appeared for my house. It was like a logjam shifting. I had been thinking of moving for years. Now I was doing it. I was house-hunting, projecting myself into different spaces, different futures, different lives. I fell in love with a flat and the life it offered me, and my proposal was accepted. I danced in the air. After two weeks of air-dancing, the sellers withdrew. That was a cliff edge and a fall I hadn't seen coming.

My sale proceeded and I decided to rent. My rental property was a treat, a charming cottage in a beautiful historic area where, for a delicious summer month, I took a holiday from life. But it wasn't home. Much of what made my home had been packed into boxes, after weeks of the most physically and emotionally tiring soul-searching, sorting and discarding. It was waiting for me in a large warehouse on an industrial estate. As the summer turned towards autumn I knew I had to get back on the street and into the estate agent's offices and find a home where I could be reunited with my possessions and where normal life, whatever that was, could be resumed.

Of course the home I found was beautiful and more than I had meant to spend. I lay awake at night in my unfamiliar bed in my rented house, doing endless mental arithmetic and staring in the dark at the terrible cliff edge of penury and homelessness that waited for me if I got this wrong.

'I must remember this,' I wrote in my diary. 'I must remember this sense of being derailed, of free fall, of losing familiar landmarks, of anxious attempts to recreate normality, or what I used to call normality.'

'What is my worst fear?' I wrote at four in the morning. And I answered myself, 'That all my sums are wrong and I suddenly find myself at the end of all my resources and unable to pay my bills. In short, I am afraid I will find myself in serious financial trouble.'

But I was afraid of much more than that. I was a creature without a home. Just because I had chosen to uproot myself didn't mean that down in the dark, away from the directing searchlight of my intellect, something smaller and more vulnerable wasn't whimpering with fear of the unknown.

Once upon a time my city was hit by a hurricane. My quiet suburban street was littered with uprooted trees and, as I stood and stared at the wreckage of the night's winds, I saw a squirrel behaving in a very unusual way. It was gibbering and squeaking and racing round and round in circles, in and out of the fallen branches. 'It's lost its home,' someone said. Of course it had. Not only had it lost its home, its world had literally turned upside down and it couldn't recognize the place any more.

Just because I had willed and planned my own dislocation didn't mean that, deep down, I didn't have an inner squirrel. Even as my adult self did calculations and talked to agents, a more primitive part of me was squeaking and scurrying in pointless circles. In the totally irrational and high-stakes business of buying a house, hysteria is never that far from the surface and must be acknowledged.

I've learned that if I take time out to listen to that inner squirrel it will calm down. So I did. I asked myself, again, what was the worst that could happen. I wasn't really homeless, not like the beggar by the cashpoint at the end of the street. I was just between homes, which was a very different thing. If the worst came to the worst and I was buying beyond my means, well, I'd just have to let the place out or put it back on the market.

My squeaky squirrel shut up. The cliff edge receded. My caravan of camels started walking into the desert again and grass sprang up beneath their feet.

A Short Guide
to the Subconscious

I believe that many projects fail because some unacknowledged part of ourselves is not on board. Jostling about under the surface of a well-ordered mind are a crowd of unexamined ideas that, collectively, can sink the proud ship of your hopes like the iceberg holing the unsinkable Titanic. It follows that if you want to change your life, it helps to become acquainted with your subconscious.

You know your subconscious mind may be operating against you when you have strange dreams. You suspect its influence when you apply your conscious mind fully to a project and yet are ineffective. You can detect its presence when you make silly errors even when you thought you were in control. It is probably no accident that you post the uncensored letter and throw your careful rewrite into the bin.

You know your subconscious mind may be operating in your favour when you suddenly put two and two together and make five. You suspect unseen forces are operating when the perfect book jumps off the library shelf. You can be sure your subconscious mind is at work when you fall asleep with a problem and wake up with a solution.

Once you become aware of the ways in which your subconscious mind works, the next step is to harness its power on purpose. I believe that we should all become skilled at connecting with our unconscious mind because the best decisions are made by a mind co-operating with itself. Here's a short history and geography of your unconscious to help you find it.

In some ways the unconscious is a twentieth-century invention. Before Sigmund Freud reached down into the dark recesses of his patients' minds, people had found other explanations for the forces of unreason in their lives. Mostly they thought of them as gods. If plans went awry, ships were wrecked and wars raged out of control that was because Apollo or Athene or Aphrodite was miffed and wanted to make things hot for humans. You could attempt to appease the gods, but they were essentially capricious. They were there to relieve you of any illusions that you were the master of your fate. They specialized in punishing hubris, the overweening pride that affects people who think that they have everything under control, with a deflating shot of nemesis, the nasty come-uppance that punishes pride in the end.

The idea of fate as an external force over which man had no control held sway for the next couple of thousand years. Then along came Freud and examined the random ragbag of contradictory ideas and symbols that came up out of his patients' minds when they stopped censoring themselves. He asked himself, could it be that we are somehow creating trouble for ourselves? Could the forces of sabotage be right inside us?

We have taken Freud's view of things ever since, more or less, though his followers, especially Carl Jung, developed and changed his ideas. Freud thought of the subconscious as a kind of cellar where we threw all the bad and inadmissible urges, particularly the sexual ones, that nineteenth-century Viennese society rejected. Jung's cellar was much bigger than Freud's and it had underground tunnels linking it up with all the other human cellars in one great collective unconscious. We weren't just driven by hidden factors in our own lives. No, we were all affected by the collective taboos of our history and culture.

The huge power the unconscious has over us comes from

repression. It is the subversive power of the hidden and unknown. The surface problem may be that you have difficulty getting a job, but your lack of success may stem from a lack of belief in your own worth, which in turn may come from messages you may have taken in and buried in your own cellar as child. And these may originate from a collective belief in your family that to rise above your station is to invite jealousy, even retribution. If you sabotage yourself, then you will not break your family taboo. That is a heavy burden to carry into the interview room.

So how do you let the light into your own unconscious? Better, how do you harness its benevolent power? A long-term approach is to consider psychoanalysis, the therapeutic method developed by Freud, but it is expensive and takes a long time. Plenty of methods of psychotherapy exist, however, which create less dependency and cost less money but still provide the space and listening which will bring unconscious fears and wishes into the light.

There are also many workshops and processes that will give you access to your unconscious mind and the more complete self-knowledge which follows. In the Hoffman Process, for example, they use the psychological model of a fourfold self: an emotional self, an intellectual self, a spiritual self and the body. When you learn to address each one in turn you see how often your internal selves are at odds, particularly the emotional and the intellectual selves. The intellectual self is often the bully shouting, 'Go on!' or 'Don't you dare!' while the emotional self hangs back and says, 'Shan't!' or 'But I'd really like to.' No action comes out of these impasses.

If you are resistant to the idea of psychotherapy or workshops but would still like to change the areas of your life that are not working, it is worth sitting down calmly and asking yourself what you have to gain from things going wrong. There is always something to be gained from staying stuck in even the most difficult circumstances. Repeated patterns create a perverse comfort, the comfort of the familiar. If bad behaviour was what got you attention as a child, then you may think bad behaviour is worth repeating as a way of making people pay attention to you.

Even if the benefits of change are obvious to the rational mind, like weight loss or a better job, don't underestimate the irrational resistance to change. If you change you could attract retribution or envy and this unacknowledged fear will make any escape attempt half-hearted. It is the power of the gods we are dealing with, after all.

The unconscious loves anything that isn't rational or prosaic. It won't give up its secrets if you harangue it, but it will respond to art and music and poetry. It likes to slip ideas into your mind when you are half-focused on something else. It loves to pop up on journeys or in idle moments, which is why some people rely on the three Bs – bed, bus and bath – as places where inspiration can strike. I would add 'beach', if you get the chance to walk on one. Beaches free the mind.

Contacting the unconscious mind can be huge fun. It is a rich and endlessly fascinating place, not just the dark cellar of Freud's speculations. There are many roads to it and the treasure we find there is our own. It can be what makes us whole.

Hanging Pictures,
Shifting Space

I've just bought a new picture. It was painted by a friend and I'd been eyeing it in her studio and when she had a show and I saw it framed and hung I decided to buy it on the spot.

I recommend buying art. It's very exciting and gives you lasting pleasure. It doesn't matter what you buy. You can start with postcards and posters, but once you get seriously hooked you realize a great truth: that whatever new object you bring into your life demands that everything changes round it.

I am waiting for my friend to bring her picture round and hang it for me, and I'm excited and apprehensive at the same time. I know that how the picture looks in the gallery isn't how it will look in my house, where it will have to live with other pictures and books and cushions and rugs. The colours of the painting are not the same as the colours that decorate my room and I can see I may have to move the furniture round. It will make the whole room look different and I will have to move other pictures to make way for it, which means I will have to change other rooms too. One small change creates a domino effect and it may take months for everything to fall into place.

It doesn't matter what change you make in your life, it will lead to others – and often much faster than you think. And the time and space at our disposal are finite. There is only so much furniture, so many clothes, so many friends and activities that we can fit in. If we acquire something without first thinking where we are to find room for it, then we are in for forced choices.

I learned this lesson in a big way when I bought a small piece of sculpture. It is a block of translucent Perspex no more than 12 inches square, but it has a force field which is much bigger than that. When I bought it I knew it needed space to be seen, but I had a big entrance hall at the time and I thought I could put it there on a plinth. I couldn't. As soon as I brought it home I could see that, small as it was, it needed uncluttered space all round it. I walked around my house room by room, carrying this demanding object and trying to see where it could live and breathe, and in the end I placed it on the mantelpiece in front of a large mirror because the mirror could absorb its force field and give every angle of it the space it needed. Now that I have moved into a small flat it sits on the window sill, where it has the whole of the outside world to breathe in.

Introducing something new – be it a picture or a new friend – is a great way to see your life in a new light and to understand what must go. Because things must go. The process of successful change is one of constant editing. I know people who never edit their lives and they build up a neglected clutter of possessions, piles of unopened envelopes and unanswered mail and trails of disgruntled friends. I know people who can't bear to throw out clothes they never wear. I have seen homes where people store old cars and toys, household equipment and broken furniture. If you haven't been to homes like this then I can hardly convey the drain on energy and spirits that they present. And invariably, the lives of the people who inhabit them are just as inert and stuck.

If you want to create change and energy in your life, throw things out. A great way to force a house clearance and a spring clean is to invite people round to your home. An even better way is to put it on the market. If that doesn't force a fresh look, nothing will. Except buying a picture.

Even as I fret about how this picture will look on my wall and wonder what it will force me to move, I am excited. I know it brings good changes with it.

What Will You
Give Up to Get?

Each change is a displacement. Something must give way to make room for the new. The protection of childhood gives way to the freedoms of adolescence, and the freedoms of adolescence are won by trading privileges. The freedoms of singledom are abandoned for the commitment of marriage. Financial security is traded for creative independence. The stimulation of the city is abandoned for the peace of the suburban garden. The joys of indolence are left behind for the self-discipline that brings good health.

Everything costs something. Even if you are infinitely rich and are simply adding one more possession to your store, you buy at the expense of indifference to what you already have. You trade houses and cars and partners, but you lose a sense of value. You lose intimacy and, often, a sense of gratitude. Only you know what price you are prepared to pay for the change you want to see.

Are you prepared to pay for change with your life? If you were a religious martyr, a kamikaze pilot, a burning monk or a suicide bomber you would be. And one of the prices you would pay, apart from your life, would be the chance to see your change happen.

Instant gratification is something that almost everyone who wants change has to give up. Many people who make the commitment to change consciously sacrifice their time and energy without the promise of quick results. Is the change you want to see so important that you are prepared to work for it all your life without reward? Are you a Nelson Mandela or a Gandhi? Some things take a lifetime and more: civil rights, the abolition of slavery, the abolition of apartheid. The reward must be in the resistance and the sense of rightness rather than the result.

Even if your change is a personal one, it may be harder to achieve than you thought. Look at the struggle so many people have, me included, with controlling their weight. In order to lose weight you have to give up far more than chocolate. You may have to surrender your idea of yourself as an expansive (yes, really), generous person who loves to eat and drink. You may have to rearrange your social life, abandon the sofa for the gym, walk a different way through the supermarket, give up your favourite forms of relaxation, find new ways of beating stress, risk offending others when you refuse their food and drink. This isn't just about willpower. You may have to change the very way you think.

Einstein famously said that a problem was not solved with the same thinking that created it. In order to change our thinking we must change our mind. In order to change our mind we must first understand what it is that isn't working. We must take out our dusty old mind and examine its contents. Old promises, unfulfilled expectations, out-of-date teaching, useless information all come tumbling out. They don't work any more. We could wait for the world to come to its senses and come back to our way of thinking or we could take a deep breath, measure our thoughts against our actions and the results they produce and be prepared to give them up.

This principle works at every level, whether an individual wants to lose weight or nations want to resolve conflict. When something isn't working it's a clear sign that something needs to give. This isn't giving up and it isn't giving in. It's simply giving, and no change happens without it.

The Swamp of Complaint

I am ashamed to admit that there have been many times in my life when I have slid into the swamp of complaint and wallowed there, croaking. The swamp of complaint is the habitat that awaits you if you are incapable of making a change. You can detect its presence by the perpetual sound of moaning. You are old enough to enter it just as soon as you are old enough to grumble, so it could be as young as five or six, but most people become familiar with the swamp when they become teenagers.

What a perfectly wonderful and hospitable climate for moaning adolescence is. Once you discover that somebody else has impossible parents, nightmare teachers and unreasonable amounts of homework then you can start wallowing in your little mudhole of a swamp together. And the more of you there are, the bigger and more comfortable the swamp is.

You could climb out of it, of course, by doing something. You could get together to make sense of the homework and you could work out a way to negotiate with your parents or your teachers, but to do that you would have to give up something nice. You would have to give up the camaraderie and the sheer comfort of your friendly, companionable swamp.

I remember a swamp of complaint I joined in one of my early jobs. We had a difficult and capricious boss whose demands kept changing and could therefore never be met. At coffee breaks and lunchtimes we huddled together and moaned. We gathered in the canteen each day and bitched obsessively about what a nightmare she was. How cosy, how friendly and bonding those lunch breaks were, as we huddled over our well-worn complaints like labourers round a campfire.

I'm not sure that it ever occurred to us young rookies to do the grown-up thing, to climb out of our swamp, think hard about what the needs of the situation were and take a responsible part in meeting or even pre-empting them. Nor did we have the experience and the skills to confront our boss calmly and in a positive spirit in order to work out a way in which she could get what she wanted – fresh ideas and diligent research – without leaving us totally frazzled. So we stuck together and complained and in due course we left, I suspect just ahead of her decision to fire us.

When change comes to a group, be it friends, family, work colleagues or even a larger political grouping, there will be people, the majority, who dive, with a splash, into the swamp of complaint and stay there, making a lot of noise. There will be those who hang back, assess the situation and adjust creatively to the new reality. There will be a smaller group of people who are really far-sighted, see a much bigger picture and decide to make changes in their turn. And there will always be the happy, far-sighted rats who already have their exit strategy for leaving the sinking ship. The swamp is really the least creative and the least energized place to be.

As I have grown older I have become much more aware of swamps of complaint and how damaging they can be to the people in them. We jump in because we are in search of sympathy, but they suck us down. Now I recognize the signs. They are: becoming conspiratorial, endlessly voicing old feelings and points, never coming to any positive conclusion, talking behind people's backs but never to their faces and voicing negative views without offering positive solutions.

I also know the best way to behave when you are faced

with change you don't like. Take time to assess the new situation. If necessary, test your understanding by spelling it out to others to get their feedback. Work out what immediate and positive steps you can take to improve things. Come up with a list of ideas and seek a meeting, though only if you know the outcome you want from it and what you are going to do if you don't get it. Work out for yourself what your bottom line is if things don't go the way you would like. Are you prepared to leave?

Above all – and this is the difficult bit – resist the temptation to moan and grumble if you don't get an immediate solution. Either keep your counsel or seek out the company and advice of wiser and more experienced people. Ask for help with real situations, not just an indulgent ear for your fears and furies.

The swamp of complaint is a most seductive place, but no

revolution was ever organized there. No great breakthrough has ever come from its depths. People who stay in swamps are overlooked and not respected. If you want to make changes, you have to climb out.

The Resourceful Mind

Someone I know is fond of declaiming that there are no problems, only solutions. This can be irritating if you're in the mood for sympathy rather than a pep talk. Nevertheless, the person in question has indefatigably built up a business which contributes to the health and welfare of poor people all over the world. He inspires and leads other people, and most people who know him would agree that, for mental fresh air, inspiration and sheer problem-solving, he is the man to turn to. He is a social entrepreneur, someone who brings about change through ingenuity and lateral thinking.

I love people who are resourceful, people whose natural response to difficulty is to see a way out. Their company clears your brain, energizes you and blows away the downward gravity of negative thinking. It helps you enjoy a wider view.

Journalism is a good training in resourcefulness because

you have to learn not to take 'no' for an answer, but journalists report on changes in the world rather than make them. When I want to rub up against people who actually solve problems I go to a meeting of a group called the Funding Network. It costs me money, because that is the reason for their existence, but I get inspiration in return.

The idea is for people to gather together to raise money for small organizations who are involved in creating social change. What is different about these meetings is that the organizations are given the space to make a pitch for funds and we get to ask them questions before we decide to hand over any money I always want to give something to everyone, because I am so inspired by the stories of people who are only there to find solutions. I learn about problems I've never dreamed of, but I realize how little it takes to make a big difference.

What I have also learned at these meetings is that I love elegant and appropriate solutions. There is a remote community in Nigeria which is being helped by a student organization called Engineers without Borders. The community lives on the far side of a river from essential services like markets and health care. People can travel in the dry season, but in the rainy season the river and its tributaries flood and the tracks are washed away, so they are marooned. They die from being cut off from medical care.

The engineering students proposed the building of five low-tech bridges which would free the community from their isolation. We gave them the money. The villagers were happy. The engineering students gained invaluable experience. A problem was solved and everyone benefited.

Another cause I liked was an equally elegant project in

which unwanted bicycles in the UK were mended and restored by young offenders in institutions, then shipped to Africa, where they provided low-tech transport for workers in rural communities. Again, everyone benefited. The young offenders learned skills, empathy for others and a pride in their work. The rural communities in Africa gained an environmentally friendly form of transport and the bicycles got a new lease of life.

The company of social entrepreneurs is addictive. At the last meeting of the Funding Network donations passed the £1 million mark after four years of private individuals donating in increments of hundreds of pounds. That's four years of a huge variety of solutions to social problems: street opera for the homeless, literacy training for South African children, education for AIDS orphans, boats for island dwellers, dance classes for socially excluded children, legal help for prisoners on death row, funding for ideas networks which will plant and water seeds for yet more positive change.

Being among people like this, both donors and doers, affects your thinking in other areas of your life. You begin to wonder what else is possible. You begin to see how situations can be turned to the good. It makes you more resourceful yourself, because you know people that you can put in touch with other people and that together they can turn a problem into a solution. And you begin to understand how a very small change can let light and energy into a seemingly hopeless situation. It doesn't have to take a Bill Gates and a billion-dollar budget. One or two committed workers with skills and a few thousand pounds can transform and empower other people's lives just as easily.

What it takes to make this kind of change, I've learned, is the willingness to stop and ask what can be done. Then you ask, 'Can I do this or do I know someone who can?' We all have something to put at the service of others – time, money, skill, experience. I have learned that the most basic gift is the willingness to believe in a solution, even if we don't yet know what it is, and to support those who might know.

Listen, Listen, Listen

My idea of hell is a place where nobody listens to anybody else. This is a place that can never change, except for the worse. It is a place where no deadlock can be broken, no fresh ideas unfold. It is a place that breeds unhappiness, rage, rebelliousness and violence.

In a place where nobody listens to anybody else, be it a home, a workplace or a whole country, individuals retreat into frustration and sullenness, and desperate citizens take the law into their own hands. In a world where nobody listens to anybody else, nations go to war. People die of collective deafness.

No good change can happen in such a place, but conversely, when people are prepared to put their egos aside and pay attention, remarkable things can happen. I once heard a man pitching for money on behalf of an African village project for AIDS orphans. The need of the children was acute and desperate. The solutions the man was offering were sustainable and cost-effective, but what impressed me most was that the whole village was involved, co-operating on a foundation of listening. No decisions about the children and their future were made without a long period of fact-finding and village meetings to make sure that everyone was in agreement.

Listening takes longer than impetuous and over-riding action, but its effects last longer. We think that democracy is the system that best ensures that everyone has a voice and is heard, but it isn't. Democracies are about majorities. They are fairer than dictatorships by a mile, but in a democracy it is still possible for presidents and prime ministers and parties to win power when nearly half the country is against them. It is very possible to live in a democracy and not be heard.

Countries are more cumbersome than committees and majorities are more practical than long consultation processes, but there are ways to communicate and take decisions in smaller groups like workplaces and families where everyone can be heard.

My friend David is a Quaker and I asked him to explain to me the attentive and deeply respectful way in which Quakers take their decisions.

First, there seems to be no desperate culture of winners and losers. Nobody is out to get their way in a meeting because the way will emerge through a collective will. In a Quaker business meeting everyone has the responsibility to listen carefully to others and not to speak just to repeat a point that has already been made by someone else. You may rise in agreement with someone and say, 'My friend speaks my mind,' but you don't go over ground that has already been trodden. Think how much going round in circles that saves.

You can only listen if you are engaged, according to David. It isn't a passive activity. And there is also a responsibility to speak your own truth. The aim is not to reach a majority decision but to arrive at a sense of the meeting. If the meeting cannot agree, the matter is postponed for further discussion at a later date. There is an underlying faith here that timing is important and that if you allow silence, listening and the passage of time their due importance, a consensus can be reached.

What I have learned about listening is that it is harder and harder for people to do. We are in the habit of not paying attention to one thing at a time. We have television and radio on constantly. There is hardly any activity that we don't allow to be interrupted by a mobile phone. We have become used to hearing the world in shifting layers and to being surrounded by sounds which we don't hear and certainly don't listen to. Time constraints mean that everyone is in a rush and people are too impatient and too unused to the art of concentration to surrender to the unhurried pace of a Quaker meeting.

But the inability to listen brings all kinds of bad consequences. Rushed decisions are often bad decisions, and people who feel disregarded and unheard are hurt people who brood and fester. When nobody listens, people go to law, and to war.

I have learned that there is no situation where people need to listen to each other that doesn't benefit from some formality. In the British parliament, where feelings often run high, the tradition is that members do not address each other directly. Instead they make all their remarks to the Speaker, a neutral figure who keeps order. It is amazing how rude people can be to each other even when they don't address each other directly, but at least by referring to each other in the third person nobody descends to personal name-calling and angry insults.

Even with children you can make a discussion into a game with talking sticks or pebbles, so that only the child holding the stick gets to speak while the others listen. This works for teenagers too and there is no reason why it shouldn't work even between couples when emotions run high.

In many situations it also helps to have a neutral person holding the space and ensuring that everyone is heard. When this isn't appropriate it helps to agree beforehand that each person will hear the other out, without interruption, for an agreed length of time. Even five minutes without interruption is enough for one person to speak and another to listen. This works even better if people agree to hold a moment's thoughtful silence before the next person jumps in.

Beware of the signs that somebody is not listening, even if they are not talking either. Look out for lack of eye contact, for folding arms, for shuffling papers. Just because somebody is in the room doesn't mean that they are paying attention.

And be aware of the effect that the act of being listened to has on you. Somebody who is really being listened to feels their pulse slowing, their thoughts coming more clearly, their spirits rising and their confidence growing. Both listener and the listened-to know what it feels like to bloom in mutual respect.

Dreamers and Stalkers

Are you a dreamer or a stalker? There are plenty of glib formulae which split the infinite complexity of human nature into two easy camps, but when you look at how people cope with change, the idea of dreamers and stalkers can be enlightening. I know. I have some of each in my own family.

Dreamers are visionaries. They are exciting and uncomfortable, inspiring and infuriating. They march to a different drum, one that only they can hear, but if you hang around them long enough you may find that you are marching to it too. Too late. They are off to the beat of another drum you hadn't even begun to hear. Sometimes they march straight over cliffs and through swamps, because heaven forbid that they should be over-cautious. They don't even open envelopes or read instructions, because they'd rather make the rules up as they go along and they hate being told what to do.

Dreamers are lateral-thinking and original. If they follow a course of action it has to be one they thought of for themselves. They can be eloquent talkers but infuriatingly poor listeners. Why should they listen? They know already. If they do pause long enough to listen to somebody else, what they hear triggers a fresh idea and they are already off on a new trail.

Dreamers can be hurt and surprised when they bump into other people's ideas and feelings. They can be so wrapped up in their own passions and enthusiasms that they just don't notice that other people have feelings too. They live in a world of their own, but talented dreamers can make you want to live in it with them because their world is an original and exciting place.

Stalkers, on the other hand, make their way through life by closely observing what others do. They want to understand the underlying rules of the situations they enter. They want to learn the language and the customs and they want to work out where they will fit in. Stalkers are born cautious, whereas dreamers have caution thrust upon them.

Stalkers are good at map-making, interpreting, managing, analysing. Dreamers blunder along, inspiring others with original ideas but seldom stopping to implement them. Dreamers are great at 'What if?' Stalkers are excellent at 'How?' and 'Why?'

Society favours stalkers because they are more easily understood and controlled. It would be much less wearing if all of us would wait to learn the ropes and proceed cautiously, but a world of stalkers would be a stagnant, stationary and hidebound place. It would be sensible but limited. A world of dreamers, on the other hand, would be like living in a lunatic asylum – everyone in a happy world of their own, unable to convey their excitement to others because nobody would be listening.

Of course, most of us are a mixture of dreamer and stalker, and we need to be. When it comes to making changes we need both elements in our personality and in our thinking. We need to dream because no change was ever made without imagination. We need to stalk because we can't take action without information.

We dream, say, that we might fly to the moon. Generations of poets and visionaries gaze from their windows and lasso the moon with metaphor and rhyme. But generations of scientists chip and claw their way towards it with observation, experiment and calculation. Imagination sets the goal, but it is information and research that get us there.

On a more intimate level, a dreamer falls in love with a pretty face. A stalker (and not in the sinister sense) finds out her name, who her friends are and whether she is available. He works out where she might like to go and what pleases her. He pays attention to her – maybe a little too much – while the dreamer is enraptured by her but maybe counts a little too much on her being enraptured by him.

On an international level, a dreamer has a vision of bringing peace where there is conflict. A stalker delves to the roots of conflict and brings together the people who have the most influence in the area so that the dreamer can entrance them with their vision of the future.

Stalking can be weary, dispiriting work. Caution and the insatiable need for yet more detail can be paralysing. Stalkers need the inspiration and the motivation that dreamers can provide, but dreaming alone can be ineffective and ungrounded. It is the dreamer who provides the electricity, but without the stalker's attention to detail the power is never earthed. If you want to make change in your own life and the wider world you must learn to dream and then to stalk. You must learn the art of dreaming with your feet on the ground.

It helps to recognize that these two sides of yourself need time and space to operate and be heard. In most of us the stalker, endlessly making lists, drives out the dreamer. But as long as it is given encouragement, the dreamer can operate at the unconscious level while the stalker is busy with the information-gathering.

You can successfully manage your dreamer and stalker by giving them both time and space. When your dreaming side feels vague and ineffective, it is time for some stalking. If you feel ground down by the minutiae of action and have lost the bigger picture, stop. It is time to unharness your mind and let it into the field of dreams. When you harness both these aspects of yourself, it is amazing what a powerful team they are. No conscious and effective change can be made without them.

The Arts of Getting
What You Want

Everyone imagines that their life would magically change if they could only get what they want. 'If only I had a job, a boyfriend, a beautiful flat, world peace, my life would be transformed.' But what if you are one of the millions of people who drift along not really knowing what it is they want, other than something different from what they've got?

Knowing what you want is the essential starting-point for making a change. It is only once you have a goal that you can shift gear and start moving towards it.

And how do you move? History records thousands of different methods, from the magical to the murderous, that people have used to get what they want. You can sacrifice animals, sacrifice your children, dedicate your herds or your crops to the gods, placate them with spilt blood. You can steal what you want, as Paris did with Helen of Troy. You can go to war, as the Greeks did in order to get her back. Woo what you want, write letters to it, besiege it, save up for it, labour for it seven years and win it by your fidelity. Seduce and cheat for it. Travel round the world in search of it and find it in your own backyard. Go on a quest to pursue it and be worthy of it and let your life pass in the quest while you forget what it was you wanted in the first place.

You can fight for it, trade for it. You can employ magic spells, ratlike cunning and feminine wiles. You can enact rituals, chant by the light of the moon and dance round fires. You can raid and kill and enslave people for it. You can go right up to someone who's got it and just ask for it. You can work and work to save up for it. You can learn the skills yourself and make it. You can marry for it and make heirs to claim it. You can go down on your knees every night and pray for it. You can study and labour and pass exams in order to qualify for it. If you have done even some of these things, I think you probably really want and deserve it.

Or – and this is just a suggestion – you can take small steps. First, be specific. Second, be positive. It is never enough to say 'I wish I wasn't here.' No energy or action can gather round something as unfocused as that, and energy and action are what you need.

Research is a big part of getting what you want. Does it really exist? Does it break the laws of physics? If it is within the bounds of physical possibility, no matter how far-fetched, then it exists somewhere and can be attained.

Desire is only the start. You don't just pray for an end to world poverty and then go back to bed. By all means declare your intention. That is a necessary and powerful thing to do. Write it on a piece of paper, put it in a bottle and throw it out to sea, pin it to a tree, fly it on a kite, write it in the sky if you want and certainly announce it on television, but that is only a beginning.

I used to go to courses at the Actors' Institute where they had all kinds of inventive ways of stimulating you to become creative and envision what you wanted. But when people had stood up and told the room that they were going to make their own movie or star in a West End show, the teachers would always say, 'And what small step can you take towards that goal right now?'

The 'now' is important because your step needs realistic timing. It is unrealistic and unsustainable to drop a clothing size in a week, but you could do it in six weeks. What is more, that is a measurable goal. Unlike world peace or the perfect home, you will know exactly when you have achieved it.

Specific. Positive. Timed. Measurable. Keep those words in mind as you get to work on that combination of the big idea and the small step. I can't get the lead in a big show tomorrow, but I can sign up for acting classes. I can't publish a bestselling novel tomorrow, but I can set myself the goal of writing 1,000 words a day and I can join a local writing group where I can read my work out loud and get feedback. I can't end world poverty overnight, but I can trawl my network of friends and acquaintances and see who would like to get together to brainstorm ways to begin. And in the meantime, here's some money for the Red Cross box.

Every wish needs a vehicle and every change needs support. The lone longing in the night can translate into a clear wish, but the wish will only be granted if you show – who? the universe?

yourself? – that you are serious. It is once you have declared your intention and started to walk towards it that you will meet the happy coincidences, the chance encounters, the surprise funding and the unexpected encouragement that reward intention and commitment. You can think of this as cosmic, or divine, if you will, and gratitude never went amiss. But your good fortune is the inevitable result of the energy you create when intent and effort meet.

A Creature of Habit

When you are little everyone wants you to have good habits. They drill them into you: clean your teeth, brush your hair, say your prayers, do your homework, say 'please' and 'thank you', clear your plate at every meal. With endless nagging, hugs, praise and punishment, we are socialized into being nice little girls and boys.

Then we make up some habits of our own. The curtains must be drawn just so. I can't go to sleep without a drink of water. Teddy must be on my left and a giant blue rabbit on my right. If the hall light isn't on I'll have nightmares. A slowly rising structure of rituals and habits keeps chaos at bay.

Habits can be broken. I bet you can sleep without a big blue rabbit now. But they can't be broken easily. In fact it's only when you try to break a quite harmless habit, like listening to a certain radio programme or always eating your apple core, that you realize it has the power of addiction.

Habits, by definition, are unconscious, which means that we probably don't even know we've got them. I've thought hard and here are some of mine. I listen to the radio as I fall asleep and then wake up in the small hours wondering why I've been dreaming about African politics. I slip small change into the pockets of whatever I am wearing so that I always end up with loads of useless coins. I carry my keys in my pocket rather than a bag, even though I shout at my daughters if they do the same thing. I always lock my front door and then realize I've forgotten something and have to go back in, no matter how hard I think before I leave my house. I make phone calls first thing in the morning, no matter what work I have to do and especially if I should be getting on with something else. I check my e-mails last thing at night. I finish people's sentences for them.

Here are some habits I have managed to break. I have cut down on drinking alcohol and realized how much I treated the first glass of wine in the evening as a demarcation and a ritual. Now I have to find something else to do that job.

Actually, I can't think of any more habits I have broken, though I do read far less addictive newsprint than I used to. When I think about it, most of the habits I have broken in my life have been simply outgrown rather than defeated. When we jettison a habit it's either because something better is on offer or because the consequences have got worse. I don't want to be laughed at when I go to big school so I'll leave my favourite blanket at home. My skirt is getting tighter, so I'll stop eating doughnuts with my coffee. But the older and more complex and layered we become, the harder and harder it is to change old habits and create new ones. The first, simplest and most difficult rule of habit-changing is simply to become aware of our habits. They are invisible to us, but easily spotted by other people, so if you want to change a habit, ask a friend to point one out.

To change a habit you also need motivation. Either a bad habit is undermining you or you want to replace it with a good habit, one that will build you up. After the decision, it is a matter of constant awareness and reinforcement. As someone once said to me, if I had to start using my toothbrush with my left hand instead of my right, it would probably take a month of transferring it from my right to my left hand before I got the new habit. Experts in behavioural change usually say that a new habit takes three months to become ingrained.

I do know that it is worth the effort. A small change in your habits can be the catalyst for a bigger change. That first change can be a step that leads in a whole new direction. Apart from anything else, it teaches you the simple lesson that you don't have to be a prisoner of your own behaviour.

Fulcrum for Change

One May morning, two months after my father's death, I sat by myself, contemplating my life, how it had changed and how I wanted it to change more, and I wrote: 'I must find a fundamental, pared-down, unchanging point of balance within myself, a fulcrum. Need this be within myself? Need I do this alone? If I didn't do this alone, how would it be?'

How is it when you want to make a change and you need help? The list I began then showed me just how many people, places and things could provide that fulcrum, that point of balance and leverage which you need for the tide to turn. A world that can seem bleak when you are at a low point is actually teeming with life. Once you lift your head to see a wider horizon than the kitchen table and the sheet of paper before you, it becomes full of places on which to stand, look back and move forward.

I wrote: 'My fulcrum could be a place, a practice, a belief, a goal.'

Stop there. What would the place be? It could be a public place, a café where the passage of people would distract me and break up my thoughts. It could be a place of information, a library or a museum where I could research an idea or a course of action or be inspired by the work of the past. It could be an art gallery where the creativity of artists could teach me to solve problems and see my life from a fresh perspective. It could be a hill, a lake, a walk in the park.

I wrote on. My fulcrum could be a star to steer by, a human example. It could be one other person, a friend or a group of friends. It could be a counsellor or a therapist. It could be a life coach. It could be a book, not just an obvious self-help book but a biography or a novel. I've just finished reading Wilkie Collins's great detective story *The Moonstone* and one of the characters, the old steward Gabriel Betteridge, treats *Robinson Crusoe* as the fountain of all wisdom. 'When my spirits are bad – *Robinson Crusoe*. When I want advice – *Robinson Crusoe*. I have worn out six stout *Robinson Crusoes* with hard work in my service.' Everyone has their own *Robinson Crusoe*.

Maybe I want to change in a way that needs rules and the support of an organization. Studies of the way in which people change their behaviour to get fit show that those who do best are supported by groups like Weight Watchers. My fulcrum could be an athletics club or a 12-step programme, a yoga class or a reading group. I know a reading group whose members have seen each other through marriage and childbirth, death and divorce.

My fulcrum for change could be a belief. It could be the practice of prayer or the support of a church. It could be a daily ritual, perhaps something as simple as lighting a candle and writing in a journal. Thousands of people have found a fulcrum for change in Julia Cameron's suggestion of writing Morning Pages, which you will find in her bestselling book *The Artist's Way*. In her experience people can write their way out of one life and into another.

Maybe I need to take myself out of my normal life altogether for a while. I could make a fulcrum of time. It could be 20 minutes to brainstorm an idea or to meditate. It could be a day off or a holiday to recharge. I could go on a religious retreat or a yoga week. I could invest in a process specifically designed to change your life, like the Hoffman Process, in the belief that it would fast-forward me away from my old habits and towards a new belief in myself. And I could come back and find that anything was possible with the support of just one person who loved me.

There are so many ways to change. First, though, you have to know you want to change. And you have to admit you want to change. And you have to commit yourself in some way to a public declaration of your intention. And then you find that if you really want to make a change, fulcrums and levers are everywhere.

New Year, Old Self

Every day can be New Year's Day if you want to make a change, and the right timing can make all the difference. I learned this the long, slow way by doing what everyone else does: trying to change my life every year on 1 January.

Self-knowledge can be very uncomfortable if you are honest with yourself, and there is nothing like keeping a diary over a period of time for revealing yourself in an unvarnished and even shocking way. I have been keeping a diary for over 15 years now. Every year I would sit down around New Year's Day in a quiet, undisturbed place and I would read through the year that had just passed. What worked? What didn't? What were the highlights? What were the lows? What was planned but unachieved? What were the unexpected pleasures, fruitful encounters, avoidable setbacks? On this basis of understanding my past year I would plan and build the next one.

Once I did something different. I sat down for a longer period and I read through ten years' worth of diaries and I was deeply sobered, so sobered that I had to laugh at myself. I saw myself through a stranger's eyes and it was a humiliating experience. I saw just how stuck I was. I saw how I began each year doggedly, blithely setting myself the same old goals. This year I was going to start the same exercise regime, this year I was going to lose the same 14lbs, this year I was going to unleash the same creativity, address the same long-standing situations, resolve the same problems. I could see I'd said the same old stuff every year for the last ten years and hadn't done it, and yet each year, like Groundhog Day, the cheery day of resolution had come round and I had made cheery resolutions.

It's a crowded place, this Groundhog Day of familiar resolution. If you doubt me, go to the gym in the first week of

January and see if you can find a spare locker.

'Don't worry,' said the gym attendant last time I did this. 'It's like this every January. By the middle of February everyone will have gone.'

Yes, and the gym will be much richer for all the fees they gather from post-Christmas fatties who last two well-meaning weeks and then quietly drop out.

It was obvious, looking back over my ten-year record, that making New Year resolutions didn't work for me. Have I found what does? If you are reading this hoping to learn that I have cracked it, have discovered a wonderful regime and dropped two stone, then I am sorry. Turn to this year's bestselling diet book. I have learned a few things, though, about New Year resolutions.

One is, New Year is not the right time to make them. The middle of winter in the northern hemisphere is a terrible time to try to change your life. Maybe if you celebrate New Year in the middle of an Antipodean summer it feels different. For us northerners, midwinter is when we were designed to behave like bears, lay down an extra layer of fat and hole up in our caves.

At this time the energy of the Earth is at its lowest, and I realized that if you want to make changes in your life it helps to harness and ride the energy that is around you. Go with the flow of the seasons. Summer is the best time to eat more lightly and get physical. And autumn, what the French call *la rentrée*, the return, is great for intellectual, creative and commercial endeavour, for gathering in and channelling your own harvest of energy built up over the summer. It is the most productive time in nature and it's a very productive time for human beings too. I've heard teachers say that the bulk of productive work is done with children in the autumn and then built on over the rest of the year.

So I've learned that a new year, in terms of new beginnings, doesn't begin on 1 January. It can begin whenever you want. Create your own. Think hard about the surges of energy and the low moments in your own particular cycle, and work with those. You can also increase your chances of success by working towards your goals with other people.

I don't make New Year resolutions in January any more, though I do set mini-goals and make mini-resolutions throughout the year. I know that I have only ever stuck to exercise in my life when I've had someone else to do it with – morning walks on the common with friends, personal training with someone who drives me – or when I've found a class that I really like – dancing with Wendy, yoga with Ken, swimming in the sea in summer, with anyone, anywhere. And I know that it's a doddle to eat fruit and salad when the weather's warm but in winter it had better be warming vegetable soup if I'm to resist the comfort of hot buttered toast.

Above all, I know that if you want to change a habit you need the true record of what your habits actually are, not what you fool yourself they are. A diary is like a mirror – not always comfortable to look into, but it will tell you the truth if you let yourself see it.

Panic and Order

If somebody offered me a time-travel ticket to the past I know where I'd go. I'd like to scoot back to the Théâtre des Champs Elysées in Paris on the night of 29 May 1913, to the first performance of the Ballets Russes's *The Rite of Spring*. I appreciate that I wouldn't be able to hear much, because the audience erupted into a deafening riot of boos and whistles and catcalls, but I would love to have been there. It's maybe the most famous first night in history and it marks one of the shoreline moments where the shocking force of the coming century, with its violent music and wilfully ugly dancing, crashed on a nineteenth-century audience in what must have felt like an intolerable assault on the senses.

Stravinsky's music for *The Rite of Spring* is one of the most exciting pieces ever written. Its driving rhythms, vivid orchestral colour and deliberate dissonance still work on an audience at a visceral level. But it was Nijinsky's choreography that really outraged the audience. They had come to the Ballets Russes for all the spectacle and elegance of the great classical ballets – girls in tutus, men in tights. What they got was dancers dressed as primitive Russian peasants, stamping and circling, feet turned inwards, heads bowed. They saw it as deliberate ugliness and perversion. They took it as an insult and roared in protest.

It is a common reaction, when confronted with something new, to feel that you are being mocked and made fun of and to react defensively, even aggressively. The new is often shocking and it often means to be. People don't get it and that makes them feel stupid and cross. This is why Hans Christian Andersen's fairytale *The Emperor's New Clothes* is so endearingly popular. People don't want to be the fawning courtiers who tell the naked Emperor how beautifully he is dressed. They want to be the little boy who calls out, clear-eyed and unashamed, 'But the Emperor has no clothes!'

I may not have been at the first night of *The Rite of Spring*, but I've had an experience like it. I have a friend who is a friend of the avant-garde British composer Sir Harrison Birtwistle. One year he was invited to write a new piece to be played at the Last Night of the Proms, one of the more conservative nights of the BBC summer season of classical concerts. We were invited along to the *tutti* rehearsal on the morning of the last night, along with the composer's family, and sat through the orchestra's rehearsal of Sir Harrison's piece for saxophone and drum soloists, called 'Panic'. It was very hard listening. When the concert was televised to a worldwide audience of millions, there was outrage. The piece was a violent onslaught on the ears and the brain. Thousands of listeners and viewers, who had tuned in to hum along to a melodic bit of Elgar, wrote in to the BBC to complain.

I have two memories of that morning. One is of the composer himself, sitting cross-legged on the floor in the middle of the empty auditorium with the open score before him, calmly following the pandemonium of sound on stage. The second is of having a coffee beforehand with him and looking at the handwritten score he carried with him and marvelling at the fact that the score itself was an object of great beauty. The music may have sounded like the aural equivalent of torn pages and blots and splashes of ink, but what was on the paper, in Sir Harrison Birtwistle's exquisite handwriting, was pure order and meaning.

I think of that score, and the violent music that came out of it, quite often. I think of it whenever I am tempted to behave like the audience at the first night of *The Rite of Spring* and boo and jeer at something which I don't understand. It's not that I liked the music – expecting to like things the first time you experience them is unrealistic – but Sir Harrison Birtwistle's score taught me that there is an underlying reason for and a thinking behind most of the changes in life which we find so shocking. Even anarchy has a philosophy.

This is not the same as saying that everything new is automatically good, however offensive we find it. Only time will tell. But stepping back, observing, listening and asking ourselves, 'If there's a reason for this shocking change, what could it be?' will have many effects. It will lessen our uncomfortable feelings of dismay. It will increase our understanding of how ideas arise. It will give us something to do other than being knocked in a heap. And it will certainly widen our boundaries of pleasure. Any performance of *The Rite of Spring* now, almost 100 years on, is bound to be a sell-out.

How to Change Your Mind

Every day I change my underwear and my clothes and I might change my hairstyle and my make-up. Not quite so often I change my sheets and towels and less often still I change the cut and colour of my hair. Every few years I change my car. You are probably not so different from me. We change our surface layers and the outer shell, but it is much harder to change the way we behave and, excuse a personal question, but when did you last change your mind?

I've often thought there should be a new kind of reality TV show, not one where they throw away the contents of your fridge and your wardrobe, but one where they scrub your prejudices and worn-out thoughts and help you think some nice new ones. It wouldn't be quite so simple and superficially transforming as getting a new haircut, but it would be much more fun.

We grow terribly comfortable with our dear old minds. It cheers us up to hug the same preconceptions tightly to ourselves, to jeer at the same politicians, to hum the same familiar tunes. There's a tribal cosiness in clinging to the same old friends who share our tastes and vote the same way we do and who make sure, by their reinforcement, that we need never think our position through on anything. Why go to all that bother when we are all speaking the same easy shorthand?

Here's why it's important to change your mind on a regular basis: because your thoughts are your interface with the world and the world is changing as you read this sentence. Because unexamined thoughts become prejudices and if you are content to live with an unexamined set of prejudices you might as well stay in bed in the morning. Because information changes all the time and we quickly become out of date. Because examining and challenging your mind keeps you alive, even as physical movement does. The more you exercise your brain, the more responsive, flexible and creative it becomes, just like your body. Because learning new information and thinking new thoughts is just so interesting. It's a way of introducing the 'wow' factor into your life on a daily basis. Because it's huge fun.

And here's how you set about changing your mind: you do your best to meet new people, ones who aren't exactly like you and who will show you a new perspective on life. You get into the habit of listening to people. You read. Anything. Everything. You take a different newspaper from time to time just to remind yourself that there are other points of view. If you don't take a newspaper, you break a habit and buy one.

You watch the news. You make yourself watch TV programmes and listen to broadcasts that you wouldn't normally choose. You go out and learn something – a language, a skill, about a period of history – in the company of other people. They will educate you as much as the teacher. When a political issue comes into the conversation, you don't say, 'I just don't get it.' You can Google it and investigate it on the internet, or pick up a book and read about it.

You go to places you might not normally go to – a theatre, a sporting event, a museum. You travel, and not just to close your eyes and lie on a beach, but to open your eyes and walk down the back streets and just notice how different people live, how they relate and what they eat.

The more you do this, any of this, the more your mind has to work with and the more connections it can make for itself. The world of the mind is a thrilling and exhilarating place. It is inexhaustible, and whatever you learn when you are exploring it you will also learn something valuable: you will learn what does not change. Like Galileo, who was forced by the Inquisition to recant his belief that the Earth moved round the sun and yet wrote, 'Still, it moves,' you will learn what your core beliefs are. You will learn the values on which you stand. You will learn who you are.

The Three Mosts

Here is a mantra to save your sanity if the pace of change ever threatens to overwhelm you: *Most things are mostly the same most of the time.* Mutter it to calm down.

It won't always work. If you are in the middle of an emergency you need to focus your whole self on survival, but once you have survived it can help to tune yourself in to the big slow rhythms of life that underlie the surface frenzy.

When I was in my twenties I landed in Ethiopia in the middle of a revolution. Ethiopia is a country like no other in Africa and no other in the world. It has never been colonized, apart from a brief period of Italian occupation and a very focused little colonial raid when British forces marched from the Red Sea to Magdala in the Ethiopian Highlands to besiege the camp of Emperor Theodore and rescue the British envoy. This lack of foreign influence means that Ethiopia is one of the many places on the globe which probably look the same now as they did 2,000 years ago. Most people travel on foot or on donkeys. Most of them wear the traditional cotton robes. There is a national food of soft bread made from a native grain, tef, which is eaten with spiced meat and vegetables. The landscape, apart from the patterns made by erosion, is unchanged. The silence of the Highlands, apart from birds, hyenas, donkeys, dogs and the wind in the eucalyptus trees, is unbroken.

And yet, when I arrived there in 1975, a great deal changed. Emperor Haile Selassie had been the ruler of Ethiopia for decades, apart from a period of exile during the Italian occupation. In the early 1970s the country had been badly affected by drought and the people had been terribly affected by famine. Nobody took much notice of the famine and the status quo was unchanged until a BBC crew arrived and broadcast its shocking images to the world. You could argue that television changed Ethiopia. In the political upheaval which followed, the Emperor was deposed and imprisoned and the country began to be ruled by a military committee called the Dergue.

The famine and the foreign aid workers who arrived to assist brought change to Ethiopia. Famine shelters and orphanages were built along the road. Relief grain flooded into the markets. Students who were little more than schoolchildren were indoctrinated with Marxist philosophy and sent out on a nationwide crusade to preach Marxism to the baffled peasant farmers. Land reform took agricultural land away from the rich families and split it up into not always viable parcels of land for the poor. My husband, going for a walk in the hills, was stopped by a student eager to practise his English who began with the question: 'Tell me, sir, what is the role of animal husbandry in a Marxist economy?'

And yet most things were mostly the same most of the time. Donkey trains and women travelled the roads, competing to see who could be loaded with the most intolerable physical burdens. Little girls walked miles for water, carrying pots that must have weighed more than they did. Camel trains came up from the desert floor to the Highlands, carrying the grey blocks of salt to be sold in the market. Baboons leaped across the road. The highway may have been churned by the wheels of four-wheel drive and vehicles, but away from the road local people crossed the mountains on horseback looking as though they had travelled from the twelfth century.

We were all living through a Marxist revolution, but most things were mostly the same. No matter who was in charge in

Addis Ababa, it would take more than political change at the top to alter the fact that Ethiopia was a very beautiful, ancient and very traditional country where most people were desperately poor and at the mercy of external forces.

At the same time as our lives seem to be in turmoil we are also part of history, which moves in different rhythms, and part of evolution, which moves very slowly indeed, too slowly for us to notice what is happening to us. Which is a blessing.

One thing that people in a changing world long for, apart from the familiar, is a compensating sense of stillness and order. Over time I've learned that this sense of order has to be found somewhere different from the ever-shifting surface of life. In my own life I find balance in what feels ageless. I have learned to seek landscapes that are elemental. I love the bewitching energy of the city and I pursue the new with as much fervour as anybody, but I need to recharge my energy among trees and grass. And sometimes even trees and grass are too high-speed. I need rock and sky and sea, even though I understand that these too are in constant motion.

It has taken me years to become skilled at this perpetual dance between change and the changeless. It is a lifetime's work, because the shape of the future and our interpretation of the present must be constantly redefined. I've learned that if life seems suddenly to go on to fast-forward, it can help to walk somewhere unchanging and tell yourself, as you focus on whatever it is that hasn't changed, 'Most things are mostly the same most of the time.' At a particularly high-speed moment in your orbit, it may be the only thought that stops you losing all perspective.

Hooray for the Away Day

A change may be as good as a rest when it comes to getting unstuck, but a holiday is much better. Sometimes you haven't got the cash or the time for a holiday and yet you know you've got to do something to break the logjam. That's when away days can be a brilliant catalyst for change.

If you don't have the away-day habit you will be astonished at how concentrated and crystallized the effect can be. The idea is to take yourself right out of your normal environment, switch off your repetitive, dreary, habitual thinking and let something new flood in.

Let me tell you about the time I went to Paris for the day with my friend Cameron. Cameron was over in London from New Zealand for two years and it turned out that he was about to go all the way back again without having ever been to Paris. Now

I know Paris quite well and I offered to be his guide over a weekend. Time whizzed by and Cameron's departure time came nearer and the weekend shrunk to a single day. What were we going to cram in?

Cameron was an engineer and somebody had told him that the stained-glass windows in Sainte Chapelle were worth seeing. He also wanted to see the Richard Rodgers/Renzo Piano-designed Pompidou Centre. I thought, jettisoning the Eiffel Tower, the Latin Quarter and the Boulevard St. Germain, that we should stick to the Right Bank, throw in the arcades of the Palais Royal and a stroll through the Marais and, of course, have a memorable lunch and dinner before we climbed back on Eurostar.

We were both intoxicated with the idea before we even met at Waterloo early in the morning. Spirits were high. We laughed a lot. I loved the fact that everything was new and different for Cameron and he loved everything, all day. We climbed out of the métro and into the illuminated gloom of Sainte Chapelle. We walked along the quais in the sunshine and found our reserved table in the Café Marly overlooking the glass pyramid in the courtyard of the Louvre. Could it have been any more Parisian?

We drank so much wine at lunchtime, looking at the sunlit prism of the pyramid, the pigeons and the crowds, that we reeled gently through the Palais Royal, found our way to the gardens at Les Halles and, along with some young lovers and a few old tramps, fell asleep on the grass. You might think that was a waste of an hour in Paris, but the very carefree insouciance of it made us feel even more cheerful.

Cameron went off to buy a set of boules to take home. We strolled through the Marais and gawped at the inside-out bravado of the Pompidou Centre, enjoyed Niki de St Phalle's twirling fountain sculptures, window-shopped and arrived at the *fin-de-siècle* splendour of the Terminus du Nord in time to have a probably superfluous supper before we crawled onto the train and nodded our way back to London.

It was midnight before either of us got home and we were physically tired but completely uplifted by the snatched, hedonistic, utterly novel magnificence of our day. Our horizons had widened, Cameron's by a whole new country and culture. Our heads had been distracted from their rut-plodding routine and filled with fresh images, tastes, sounds and memories.

Best of all, our idea of ourselves had changed. From being desk-bound wage slaves we were suddenly the sort of people who would dash off to Paris for the day. We had mythologized ourselves into bigger, brighter beings. Like Bogart and Bergman, we would always have Paris.

The effects of this piece of rut-jumping glittered for weeks and I still get a warm glow when I think of it now. If you need to change your mood, do something unreasonable. Don't take Prozac. Jump on a train to somewhere you've never been before and change your idea of yourself.

Reading the Runes

The worst place for understanding how things are changing is at the very centre of events. It's the person on the ground who understands the rhythm of the roller-coaster. If you're on one, the best you can do is scream.

I once woke up to the crashing sound of metal and a great jolt and found that the car I had been driving through a quiet country village had somehow crashed into a car parked at the side of the road, driving it forward through a garden fence and over a wall so that it now stood on its nose in the garden below. I was unhurt but utterly bewildered.

The owners of the house, the garden and the wrecked car were white-faced and shocked because they had been enjoying a peaceful Sunday afternoon at home until a big bang had brought them rushing to their door. I was white-faced and shocked because I remembered feeling sleepy five minutes earlier and I remembered turning to drive up the hill and then I remembered nothing more.

Events like these, seemingly out of the blue, are very shocking indeed. Fortunately nobody was hurt, but our lives were all changed in an instant. The children who lived in the house could no longer get to school. (They were thrilled.) The mother could no longer get to work. (She was amazingly nice about it.) And I found myself in one of those car-crash moments in life, the ones where you were speeding forward but suddenly find all your plans suspended while you wait for the emergency services on the real or the metaphorical roadside of life.

These moments crop up through life and you can often only see them coming once they're over. As Alexis de Toqueville said about the French Revolution, 'Never was such an event so inevitable yet so completely unforeseen.' Inevitable and completely unforeseen events trip us up constantly, from the global to the personal level.

When two planes flew into the Twin Towers on 11 September 2001, the world froze in shock before its television screens. The event was unimaginable and incomprehensible and yet, as the days went by, it seemed that it had been both imagined and comprehended. Intelligence had been ignored and information discarded because it didn't fit a known pattern. Blind eyes had been turned on disquieting but unclear signals. The further away from the event we travel in time, the further we can see that its roots stretched below the cultural and political soil. People had ignored the writing on the wall.

There is nearly always writing on the wall. Coming events cast shadows. When the husband disappears or the wife leaves home, a frantic scrabbling in the rubble of the broken relationship usually brings up clues that had been overlooked in the profound desire for life to continue as it had always done.

I myself have a great capacity to manipulate the facts of my own life into a truth that suits me. If a little event or a chance remark doesn't fit the pattern that I have chosen for myself, then I ignore it. I hope it will go away.

Wilful blindness is a common reaction to coming change, especially when you are at the heart of it. That's where the Greek chorus comes in. In ancient Greek tragedy, the protagonists stumble around in the darkness of their own desires and actions, sleep-walking their way towards blindings, banishment, destruction and death. And, walking right alongside them, comes the chorus. 'This is bad. She shouldn't do this. No good will come of it. Oh dear. Too late now. Told you so,' chants the chorus. Like Cassandra, the cursed prophetess of the Trojan Wars, the chorus has the role of telling the truth and being ignored.

There is probably a Greek chorus near you right now. Its members don't speak, because nobody likes to be the bearer of bad news. Besides, they know you wouldn't listen. They are there, nodding and keeping quiet, when you make the bad choices in your life. They know that fate is closing in on you. Your friends, colleagues and family could probably tell you where it will all end, but only the brave ones do. Besides, never underestimate the optimistic desire inside all of us that things will go well despite the odds.

There is a Greek chorus inside us too. At the heart of our own darkness there is a voice that is telling the truth and not being listened to. At the wheel of my own car I knew I felt sleepy but I didn't stop. Before I got into the car I knew I was tired and doing too much. Before I even planned the journey I could have realized I was trying to cram too much in, but I thought I could get away with it. How many stressed, tired people drive about when they shouldn't and yet avoid accidents? How many people cut corners in their lives? How many people, everywhere, every day, get away with it?

And yet the runes are there to be read. And it's not that we can't read them, it's that we choose not to. If we read and acted on them we would be faced with hugely inconvenient and difficult choices. We would have to change our plans, confront the boss, act on the intelligence. So we ignore them. And we get away with it – until the day when we don't. And when we look back at the moments of choice, the writing on the wall was flashing away in brightest neon.

The wreckage of predictable but unforeseen disaster is, however, a hugely creative, life-changing place to find ourselves in. We are incredibly aware. We see where we went wrong in the marriage and promise that it won't happen again. We curse ourselves for cutting financial corners and resolve to take control. We see the mushroom cloud and set up the United Nations so we need never, ever go to war again.

These moments of shocking revelation don't hold their power forever, but for those who seize them they can be a huge turning-point. If, on the other hand, you blame everyone but yourself, you will learn nothing from them.

As for me, I climbed out of the wreckage of my car shocked and chastened, grateful to be alive and willing to rearrange the life I'd still got.

The Long Goodbye

Everything in the way we live in the twenty-first century is designed to distract us from the great void of mortality. We are urged to come to terms with, get over, move on from, deal with and deny anything puzzling, mysterious and emotionally difficult, especially death.

Those of us who have a religious belief and practice have a structure and tradition within which to contemplate death, but millions of people don't. Funerals, the one point in life where it is hard, you would think, to deny the power of death, are becoming secular to the point of being cheerfully upbeat. 'This is a celebration of life,' people say, buttoning their stiff upper lip and tuning their guitars, 'rather than a time for weeping and wailing.'

I would like to know what is wrong with weeping and wailing, not to mention the rending of garments and gnashing of teeth. Weeping and wailing may be just what we need. If you haven't howled and sobbed over the death of somebody close to you, then howling and sobbing are waiting for you somewhere ahead on the path and maybe when you least expect them. Death will not be denied.

I have learned that unacknowledged and unmourned loss is likely to express itself in different ways. The effort of toughing it out and denying that it even exists can build emotional scar tissue that deadens our sense of what we really feel. Or the grief from past wounds may break the surface of the scar tissue and surprise us when we least expect it, demanding to be felt and honoured. Either way, suppressed grief leads to a loss of self-knowledge, a deadening of sympathy with others and a numbing of our connection with our own heart.

I was at a funeral recently which made me think more about all this. We were there to say goodbye to an old friend, former colleague, husband and father. He was a hugely gregarious, life-loving and hospitable man and the tone of his funeral was very warm and affectionate. A guitarist played. People laughed at the anecdotes and remembered him with love. And yet I felt there was an elephant in the room. Something enormous had happened. Something enormous always does happen when someone dies. We were sitting there in the face of a great mystery and somehow the mystery was not spoken of.

And then, at the very end, a poet stood up. Thank God for poets. This is exactly why we need them. He read not his own work, but a poem by Brian Patten called 'How Long is a Man's Life?' As he read its searching lines on the meaning of life and the nature of immortality I felt that the real loss was being addressed.

The poet was Roger McGough and when I talked to him afterwards he said he had a poem of his own about death, one in which he stood against cheerful denial:

Don't dwell on my past but on your future.
For what you see is what you'll be,
And sooner than you think.
So get weeping. Fill yourselves with dread.
For I am not sleeping. I am dead.

Weeping is the right response to death. And in life we have to learn to live with the paradox that whenever we make a change, even if that change is longed for, there may be a death in there somewhere.

Faced with death and loss, people are often afraid to begin

grieving because they are afraid they will never stop, but you can only cry for so long. It is often only in the falling apart that you can begin to rebuild and start a fresh cycle. Then you might become one of the thousands, even millions, of people who would say that the loss which was the worst time of their lives became the motivation for the greatest and the most creative change.

Doing Nothing

I know people who choose to do nothing. Sometimes I do nothing myself, on purpose. The important thing is to do nothing consciously. If you choose to do nothing as a deliberate personal stand against the unconscious frenetic activity of the world, then the vacuum you create can do all kinds of good. The nothing can be something after all.

Doing nothing is a provocative act. It can shock and annoy people, especially people brought up in a driven Protestant work ethic. I met a woman only yesterday and I asked her, semi-consciously, the fail-safe social question, 'And what are you doing these days?'

'Nothing,' she said, shamelessly. 'I've done nothing for some time and I like it. My friends are all shocked. They say, "Aren't you working?" But what's so great about work? I think it's really over-rated.'

I know you are probably reading this and thinking, 'But what about money?' But sooner or later money can often be found for a spot of doing nothing that is both more and less than a holiday.

The opportunity to do nothing often happens when people change jobs or are made redundant. When redundancy strikes I've noticed that people react in two ways. Either they hit the phones without pausing for breath, convinced that if they don't find another job immediately they never will. Or they see a blessed opportunity, the chance to create a little vacuum of inactivity and rest, a breathing space where there was none before.

The decision to do nothing is, in itself, a major change. From birth onwards we are driven from achievement to achievement.

Reading, writing and arithmetic are constantly tested. There is even pressure on children nowadays to listen to music in the womb and learn from flash cards from birth. Their parents worry about them getting into the right school. If they are middle class, their do-nothing hours, so useful for growing and unravelling, are crammed with more activities, sports and ballet and music. The nothing times that children need to sit and dream in are dusted aside by fear of the future.

What happens when you do nothing on purpose? In my experience you usually like it a lot to begin with. The relief of waking up in the morning without a 'to do' list or an engagement diary is delicious. You make friends with time. Each necessary and gentle activity in your day is allowed to expand to its natural length. Unhurried, your wishes and desires float to the surface, some of them to be explored, some to drift away. You may get bored.

Boredom is good. It teaches you what you would rather be doing.

One of the vows in the Hippocratic oath is to do no harm. If you ally this with the concept of masterly inactivity you come up with the idea that sometimes it is better to do nothing than to do something at all costs. Sometimes, when you do nothing, problems resolve themselves, medical conditions disappear, people sort themselves out without you. When you do nothing you can become a sounding-board for other people's dreams and worries and the very fact that you have time to pay attention can help them.

Doing nothing will certainly put paid to some illusions. You may have told yourself that you would clear the cellar, plant a herb garden or write a novel if you had time. You find that you don't.

You may find that you are one of those people for whom a

period of doing nothing acts as a welcome hiatus in a busy life. It gives you time to rearrange and discard mental and physical clutter. It gives you space to dream and a welcome break from the drive to impose yourself on life.

You also learn what doesn't happen when you do nothing. Life doesn't stand still. The world keeps turning. The seasons keep passing. The lives of those around you keep dancing and reforming and maybe one day, it could be a week away, it could be a year, you will feel the need to rejoin the dance. It could be a different dance or it could be the same dance, re-energized. You will never know until you try.

But maybe you will decide to keep right on doing nothing. I have friends like that. Doing nothing, in the world's eyes, doesn't make you a nothing. It makes you enviable, a still point in a turning world. The world of paid work doesn't account for all of us. There is always plenty to do if you want to. You may find that the frugality and simplicity of your reduced material life is fully repaid by the time you now have for friendship and family and for new, non-commercial ways of contributing to your world. By the simple act of doing nothing you represent an alternative view of life which can change the world by its silent statement. In your own person you let the people you meet know that they don't have to keep running. They don't have to be driven by getting and spending. There is another way to experience life.

The Magic Wand and the Seven-Year Apprenticeship

All myths and fairytales are about the same thing: they are about change. They are mainly about two kinds of change: the kind we long for and the kind we undergo.

On the one hand, we are enchanted by the idea of magical change, the change that comes with the wave of a wand. How glorious life would be if a fairy godmother could whisk her way into our kitchen and turn the pumpkin into a brand new car or our jeans into a designer dress. The nearest most of us come to realizing this instant transformation is the purchase of a lottery ticket.

Magic-wand change is so beguiling and so effortless that it dazzles our eyes and blinds us to what the myths and fairytales are really telling us about the human condition. Which is that change can take years. Cinderella may get her invitation to the ball, but her handsome prince comes only after years of patient, good-humoured suffering in the kitchen. Beauty must sacrifice her happiness and her homesickness to stay with the Beast before she learns that he is an enchanted prince. Virtue is rewarded, but only after years of trial and tribulation.

If heroines must suffer before their fortunes are transformed, heroes must wander and work, struggle and fight. The hero's journey takes him into the underworld and through the enchanted forest. He has to overcome monsters, answer impossible riddles and negotiate labyrinths. This takes years. His life is difficult. He must struggle and persevere.

The reward at the end of all of this is not always what it seems. The hero may begin the story as a penniless youth seeking fame and fortune and he may end it with a golden crown, but the prize is more subtle than that. Along the way, the heroes and heroines of myths and fairytales must learn patience and compassion. They will be humbled as well as elevated. They will have to show self-mastery as well as quickness of wit. They will have to learn to stop and help others as well as pursue their own goals. Their rewards will be love and wisdom as well as wealth and worldly success. And love and wisdom never come with the flick of a magic wand. They must be earned.

What do myths and fairytales have to teach us about making changes in the real world? I think they teach us that we all have to serve an apprenticeship, even if we don't serve just one master.

This is not a lesson that you will find in the contemporary fairytale world that is reality TV. Reality TV offers a fairytale vision of life which is firmly in the magic-wand school. Fairy god-mothers in the guise of life coaches and style gurus and interior decorators fly in with a checklist and a budget and a team of elf-like helpers. They change the surface of things, but that isn't real change, no matter how gratifying the moment of transformation.

Real life is too slow for the cameras to capture. Qualities like self-discipline and perseverance don't translate into prime-time TV. The business of making change in real life can be draining and discouraging and lonely, which is why, when we hit a slow patch, it can be fun to mythologize our own lives. Then myths and fairytales give us metaphors for our own experience. A difficult meeting with the boss is bearding the ogre in his den. Turning bad situations into good is spinning straw into gold, a very useful skill in daily life. Malicious and obstructive people are wicked witches, but we don't have to stay under their spell.

Above all, myths and fairytales, unlike reality TV, can

teach us to have patience and never be fooled by appearances. It is a favourite trick in fairytales to disguise wisdom in rags and royalty in poverty. The true hero and heroine have to learn to pay attention to the mean and the overlooked. They have to learn to really listen to those without obvious power. Fairytales teach the arts of alliance, not alienation.

In life, at the end of apprenticeship the reward isn't always as obvious as a bag of gold. The truest reward is happiness, and that comes from overcoming difficulty and learning to see the value of what is at hand. And that is magic.

The Research and
Development Fund

Big companies have research and development funds. Individuals seldom do, but without a research and development fund it can be difficult to change your life.

I think the single most valuable thing that money can buy, apart from health, is the time in which to have a life-changing experience. I don't simply mean time learning new skills and acquiring knowledge, though this is a wonderful thing and I can never have too much of it. I mean time in which life itself can teach you.

There are changes which happen in a heartbeat, but considered change takes time. And it often takes money. Here is a dream situation. You have worked steadily for some time and you have built up a reserve fund which will allow you to take time out of your career to retrain, or to follow a passion, or to volunteer in a field that interests you, or to travel in pursuit of a dream. Of course you might have cleaned up on the stock exchange instead, won the lottery, backed a winning horse or inherited a large sum of money from a distant relative. These are all possible, but I really don't recommend counting on any of them. Creating your own fund is the way to go, but create it with a purpose. Know what it is for.

A research and development fund can buy you books that will help you change your life. It can pay for you to take an evening class or go on a weekend course, even take a part-time degree. It can allow you to travel and explore, not just to take a holiday but to travel with a purpose, to research archaeology, practise a foreign language or do voluntary work that will help someone else and re-educate and re-energize you. More and more employers are recognizing that staff who take time out to re-energize themselves re-invigorate the workplace too. A research and development fund can pay for a whole year off when you wake up and realize that you've been doing the same job without a break for far too long.

When I was 50 my research and development fund rescued me from an intolerable feeling of being stuck and sent me off to art school. When I look back at my diaries I can see that those first few weeks of art school brought me alive again. I was thrilled with the stimulation, the tapping of latent creativity. I loved the sociability of working alongside other people whose minds and spirits and lives were in a state of flux. I loved being taught how to see again. My research and development fund bought me new friendships as well as time away from my habitual life, a new level of knowledge and expertise and, in due course, new paid work.

If you are poor to start with, or young, which often amounts to the same thing, there are other ways to create the leverage which brings change in a research-and-development kind of way. You can try stepping stones *(see page 45)*. I know, for example, someone who was determined to get into radio. She had a job as a newspaper reporter which had begun to bore her and she'd done an evening class in radio which had inspired her. Against the advice of her family she threw up her job so that she would be free to do unpaid volunteer work in community radio and unpaid work at her local radio station. She earned her keep by spending nights working in a bar and cut her expenses by taking a bed in a shared room in a shared house.

It all looked grim to begin with and she worked very hard, but over the course of a single year she began to get paid shifts in radio and progressed to the point where she was doing so many of them that she could give up the bar work. Then she moved from paid shifts to a short-term contract and finally became a member of staff, earning double what she had been getting in her newspaper job and becoming more skilled because of the invaluable technical training she was getting. There were plenty of risky points along the way, but this girl created her own fund of time and effort and her commitment impressed her future employers so much that eventually she benefited from the organization's research and development fund and not her own.

Research and development may not even need a fund. It can happen in very small spaces if it must. Julia Cameron, in *The Artist's Way*, recommends artists' dates, weekly outings where you go alone into the world, take the pressure off yourself and stimulate your imagination. You could take a walk in the park, go to an art gallery or spend an hour on the beach.

I know an editor who makes all her staff stay at their desks through the lunch hour. Nobody likes working for her and their creativity and enthusiasm dry up. I know another editor who hates to see her staff at their desks in the lunch hour. She wants them out on the street seeing the latest art exhibition, picking up ideas from what people are wearing and checking out the shops. She's not daft. That is all research and development. And it not only keeps her and her staff in touch but also keeps her magazine on the ball.

Left alone, doing the same thing over and over, we stagnate and freeze. If life isn't changing for you then it is vital to create the conditions for change yourself. Having a research and development fund of your own, whether it is £50 or £500, is the best way I know of being your own guardian angel.

Children Change Everything

When I ask my friends what is the biggest change they have known in their lives they don't say the fall of the Berlin Wall or the invention of the mobile phone. They don't mention cheap air travel or global warming. They don't say the rise of Islamic fundamentalism or the joy of the iPod. They say, 'Having children.'

Having children changes everything. It is like a new planet appearing on the horizon. Everything in your world shifts on its axis and realigns itself to take in the newcomer. Your relationship with the baby's other parent changes to accommodate the new pressures on your time and energy and the new call on your heart. Your parents morph into grandparents and you see them in a whole new light. You suddenly see your home completely differently, as a container which must be made welcoming and safe. Your social life changes utterly, however much you want to pretend that everything will stay the same. The world reforms beneath the buggy wheels. Places you have never been before suddenly welcome you. Places you are used to entering freely suddenly become inaccessible. You can feel included in a new way and excluded in a new way several times a day.

The future rewrites itself. Your finances suddenly demand urgent attention. Your career must take the needs of your child and of yourself as a parent into account. Your own childhood suddenly surges up from the depths of your memory as you begin to create a childhood for your own child. Your world shrinks to the space of your own home, the space between your arms. Your world expands to a future where you will be gone but your child will live on.

Your politics may change. You will become newly impassioned about health care and education. You will begin to worry about schools and day care. Your single life with its shopping expeditions and drunken nights will disappear over the horizon. You will become newly amazed at the heedless selfishness of young people. You will discover a new camaraderie among people you hadn't previously noticed, people whose lives revolve around caring for others. You will find yourself emotionally vulnerable to other people's feelings. If you see people suffering on the news, especially children, you will be moved in a way that you weren't before. The cocoon of happy indifference and self-absorption which walls in the young and single has been breached. You are not just joined to your child. You are joined to the world through your child and that is different.

Common wisdom says that this life change is a glorious thing. Having children is the culmination of biological destiny and social and spiritual purpose. There is supposed to be no happiness like it and the childless are excluded from the very gates of heaven, an idea which only makes infertility harder to bear. This isn't the whole truth.

All change can be painful, and the arrival of children is a huge change on every level – emotional, mental and practical. For some people, especially women, it can be simply too much to bear.

Some new mothers, very few, are inflicted with post-natal psychosis, a madness which is triggered, nobody can quite agree how, apart from chemical imbalance, by childbirth and which can only be treated in hospital. It is inexplicable, it can be cured and it doesn't necessarily return with the birth of a second child, but it is devastating. Post-natal depression, which is far more common, an effect of exhaustion, hormonal turbulence and the shock of the change, can also make the early times with a new baby hard to bear. And the misery is compounded by guilt because everything isn't suffused with the promised love and light. Post-natal depression also needs medical help.

I had a neighbour who suffered from post-natal depression. She would call at my house each day and cry and wonder where her wonderful single life had gone. She had run a company, but she didn't feel ready for the responsibility of a baby. Her boundless energy turned into exhaustion and fearfulness, and her capacity for vision and drive deserted her. She got better. Most people do, but huge adjustments have to be made. It is not surprising that when your world shifts on its axis not everything falls back into place right away.

The adjustment required is much greater than it used to be. Women nowadays have more options than their mothers and grandmothers, and children can come as a huge shock. I remember interviewing a high-flying woman who had just very publicly announced her resignation as the boss of a radio station in order to stay at home with her new and wonderful baby. A few months down the line from this renunciation she was sitting in her lovely house staring out of the window and wondering how she could get back into the world of work.

Everyone must work out their own salvation. Sometimes this takes daily adjustment, but that's how it is. Stay flexible. Enjoy the moment. Above all, enjoy your children, because they change by the minute and they will soon be gone.

Children come. Your personal planet spins. The skies around you quiver and shift. Your map rearranges itself and then, slowly, the stars resume their courses. The best result is that everyone is still happily on board.

A Measuring Place

I was walking by the sea the other day with my mother and an old friend of hers. The weather was changeable. We'd sat in the car staring at tumbling grey waves through a moving film of rainwater and now the clouds had hurtled eastward and cleared a pale blue space just wide enough for a sunlit walk on the clifftop. A little town shone in the sunlight on a nearby headland and, far out to sea, a mirage of light glittered and shifted on the waves. I have known this place my whole life.

As we walked, I tempered my stride to the pace of the two 80-year-olds who were thinking and feeling their way over the uneven sheep-cropped grass, avoiding the rough patches, poking their way forward with the help of a stick. My mind suddenly shifted backwards to a day, 20 years earlier, when I was walking on exactly the same cliff edge with my grandmother and my aunt and uncle, and I realized that my mother, in her pale coat, her hat and sunglasses, now looked exactly like my grandmother had then – thin, white and erect. Both were steely wills in frail, ageing bodies, measuring themselves and their steps against the same ancient rocky landscape.

On that day, decades earlier, my grandmother and my white-haired uncle had walked slowly together while my energetic impatient aunt and I had kept slowing down to stay with them. My aunt had admitted to me that sometimes her patience ran out and she wondered what she was doing with these old people.

And, as I remembered that, my mind shifted to another day on the same stretch of coast only five years before, the day of my aunt's eightieth birthday. I was walking on the beach with my parents, seizing an hour before we turned up at my aunt's surprise birthday party. It was a glorious, poignant day. The tide was far out, leaving a great expanse of hard, gleaming sand. A glittering line of breaking waves creamed in and retreated and we all walked barefoot in the ripples, as we had since we were children.

I had a camera to snap my parents walking ahead of me, my father on his stick, my mother newly diagnosed with cancer but looking youthful in her rolled-up trousers and bare feet. I snapped away thinking, 'They might never be here again, never together.' They smile at me, sunlit, out of those pictures. My father is dead now and my mother has morphed into my grandmother. My aunt has died too.

My mind went back again to other days on the beach. There were plenty of days when I was an ecstatic, scampering child clambering on the same rocks, digging in the same sand, poking sea anemones in the same rock pools, jumping, jumping,

jumping in the same waves while the indulgent, cheerful figures of my grandparents and aunts and uncles sat on the rocks with the picnics and dry towels.

And I carried on walking in the present, along the cliff edge where the rocks were crumbling and falling into little coves and the seascape was unreeling into the past and the two old figures with me were walking with the memory of their much younger selves. Those younger selves would arrive at the beach with their bicycles and picnics. My mother would recklessly climb these cliffs as a child, as free and heedless as a monkey.

'Where?' I asked her.

'Oh,' said her 83-year-old self, 'over there where the stone wall comes down but the cliff has fallen. It's not exactly as it was.'

Nothing is exactly as it was. The whole cliff face is falling. There are signs now warning you to keep away for fear of falling rocks. I think of it as a slice of eternity, the steady backdrop to my family's mayfly existence, but it is changing too. It is simply changing at a much slower rate. Like my family, it is slowly collapsing and crumbling. Unlike my family, it is not simply the carrier of some essence, the members of a lineage who perpetuate each other, if not themselves. The cliff is crumbling into the voracious sea and will change into sand.

As I walked along it that day I remembered seeing my daughters walking the same path at that gawky teenage stage where people may be beside you in the flesh but they wish they weren't and they withdraw into an inner landscape of their own. And I remembered observing them at those many moments when the inner world pulled more strongly than the outer one, and knowing that the landscape and the sea and even the family would pull them back. The changeless world can encompass many human changes.

Finally, we turned back. The 80-year-olds were tired and we had to retrace our steps to the car. We had somewhere else to go. We were here, in my native territory, to make a visit to a very new member of the family. He was only four weeks old and he didn't know where he was yet. My cousins and I had already agreed that we wanted to be there on the day that the new arrival made his first visit to the beach by the cliffs which was the setting for so much of our own childhood happiness. This was the beach where we took our own children with sandwiches and towels and buckets and spades, but also with memory and a sense of ceremony and ritual.

Everyone should have a changeless place, a cliff edge in time and space against which they can measure the imperceptible changes of their own life. I suddenly remembered another warm summer evening when I and my grandmother had come to the beach together. I had been pregnant with my first child and had longed to walk into the water and swim. My grandmother must have been about as old then as my own mother is now. She had sat on the rocks in her coat and hat and watched as I walked into the water in my loose smock, because I had no swimsuit. Inside me, my daughter was swimming in her own inner ocean.

'We are weather,' my present self thought as I walked. 'We are weather on the surface of the Earth.' It wasn't a sad thought. There was a comfort in feeling part of an ever-changing dance that stretched backwards and forwards in time. I knew that, even as the new baby replaced my cousins and me on the sands of our childhood, I was slowly becoming my own mother and my children were slowly becoming me. Released from the pressure of being a solitary and unstable 'I', I felt the infinite comfort of being a molecule in a never-ending chain reaction.

Playing Many Parts

My mother was setting off on a train to attend a friend's birthday lunch and she was working out her outfit. My mother may be in her eighties, but she loves to dress up. She is incapable of being careless or sloppy and she soon had her birthday lunch outfit planned and accessorized from the colour of her lipstick to her elegant summer sandals. The day was changeable, sunny but cool, and I worried that she wouldn't be warm enough. 'Wear layers,' I fussed. 'Take a shawl. And a raincoat. And maybe you should have an umbrella. And it might be wise to wear a vest under your dress.'

The next day I overheard my mother, who had managed to survive, talking to friends about her day out. 'You know,' I heard her say, 'when your daughter turns into your mother?'

We do. We turn into our mothers, and our fathers. It is

their guarantee of immortality. Human beings are infinitely mutable. As Shakespeare said, 'Each man in his time plays many parts.' It seemed I had morphed into my mother's mother without noticing (though she had noticed). Whose were the words coming out of my mouth as I tried to send her into the world wrapped in cotton wool? They weren't just words she had used many times to me (though they were), they were tribal words. Generations of mothers and daughters and grandmothers stretch back into history, warning each other to wrap up warm and beware of the sabre-toothed tiger. It doesn't matter how annoying you find their advice as a teenager, because I promise you this: one day these words will come from your mouth. You will have changed roles.

Although people can get stuck in family roles – the clever one, the pretty one, the black sheep – I think we should all derive comfort from the infinite number of ways in which we swap places with each other.

It is not just within families. When I was an editor there was a bright little assistant called Nicola. She was in her first job but you could see that she had what it took. You usually can. In time she became a successful editor and I went freelance and then she became my editor and told me what to do, which was great by me.

One of the secrets of good relations, inside families and out, is to deal with others in a spirit of respect and good manners, no matter who or what age they are. Never abuse a position of authority, if you happen to have one. It's even more important to behave well when you have power because life moves on, you may change places and you will see your own words and example come right back to you. If I was being solicitous with my mother it was because I had learned solicitude from her. If Nicola is happy to work with me now, I hope it's because I was once happy to work with her.

This benevolent chain of change has an opposite, of course. It's called getting a taste of your own medicine. When people have been slighted and abused, they are rarely kind when the ball is in their court. If you terrorized your children, you don't want to be at their mercy when it's time to be bundled off to the old people's home.

This I know: in the course of a normal life we all change in relation to the people around us. Sudden wealth or redundancy, sickness and health, better and worse send us whizzing up and down the ladders and snakes. Luckily for my mother, she taught me to be kind, even if she also taught me to be bossy. And I am kind to my own children not just because I love them but because I hope that, one day, they will be kind to me.

My mother is still my mother, by the way. There are times when I still feel 12 years old in her house.

Changing roles is very healthy. What isn't healthy is to become stuck, especially when the role reversal is out of synch. I remember my small daughter apologizing to me for upsetting me by crying.

'That's OK,' I said. 'I'm here to look after you, not the other way round. You cry if you need to.'

I still remember the look of relief on her face.

The Art of Self-Reinvention

They taught me mathematics at school, and Latin, litera-
ture, chemistry, geography and physics, but no school, not even
Hogwarts, where transformation is a daily lesson, ever teaches
the essential art of self-reinvention.

If only they'd taught me, as I wrestled with 'What I Want
to Be When I Grow Up', that you don't have to be only one thing.
Not only that, you don't have to settle in only one place. You don't
have to have only one job. You don't have to speak only one language
or have only one hair colour or play only one instrument. You can
be a constantly changing narrative of your own invention. You
can be a multi-faceted, multi-skilled, complex, rainbow-hued,
mercurial shape-shifter if you want. And even if you don't want,
life may require it of you.

Nothing sharpens the CV-writing mind as keenly as the

necessity of moving on, which is the mother of all self-reinvention. The sack and the divorce, once you've got over the shock, can be recast from disaster to huge opportunity to create another self, one which you've always rather wanted to be.

It's good to self-reinvent when you are young, because life hasn't defined you too sharply. And it's good to self-reinvent when you are older, because you have so much more material to play with.

The key jargon words are 'transferable skills'. I long ago passed the point where I realized I had somehow cultivated a whole garden of select facts about myself which I could cut and present like a custom-made hand-tied bouquet to any potential taker. Who do I want this person to think I am today? Am I going to emphasize my managerial-editorial-creative-artistic-musical-committee-member self? Do I emphasize all the travelling I've done (even though a lot of it was on holiday)? Do I make as much as possible of that newspaper job (glossing over the fact that I only had it for six months)? Do I knit together the experience I've had in fashion and design to make it look like a sustained and grounded career? Do I represent the accumulated years of acquaintanceship in my address book as a valuable network of contacts?

I do believe that we all have more to offer than we think we do. As a wild exaggeration, ambitious men tend to overpolish and overplay their hand. Women tend to self-deprecate. Neither is necessary. Self-reinvention, like moving around the furniture, is a skill you practise all your life, and, in case you've got the wrong impression, I don't mean telling lies. Lies will find you out. I once read the highly embroidered CV of a secretary I worked with and you would have thought that she single-handedly made editorial decisions and upheld staff morale, when all she did was answer the phones and dispense coffee and sympathy. Still, hats off to her for sheer chutzpah.

Self-reinvention is an act before it becomes a story you tell others. It might need the conscious effort of acquiring an extra-curricular skill that you think would come in handy, but often it is done unconsciously through sheer *joie de vivre*. I think about the girl who learned Farsi for the intrinsic fascination of it and found herself working for a human rights organization in Afghanistan. I think of my mother, who has been a lifelong and devoted member of the Women's Institute and was commissioned to write a book about it, so she became an author in her seventies. I think about the friend who was a keen amateur musician for years and, when she lost her corporate job, moved into music management. I think about the friend who combined a keen interest in gardening with her experience in journalism to edit a gardening magazine and who is now the curator of a historic garden. It wasn't the linear career she planned when she first started planting her roof garden, but it's a fascinating life.

So, reinvent yourself. Do what you love. Move in the direction that draws you. Do something because you really want to. You can't lose. Your passions can become useful to you in surprising ways.

And each time you have to reinvent yourself you will find that the life you have lived is every bit as important as the job you have been paid for. What lies behind successful self-reinvention is the act of giving value to everything you have done.

Destination Sickness

You long for a change. You work and plan for it, spend months, even years, researching, wheeling and dealing. You dream and study and sacrifice and then you get it. The thing that was going to change your life forever is now yours and you can allow yourself to overflow with the champagne intoxication of homecoming.

And then. You wake up feeling flat. The calm happiness that follows ecstasy has somehow ebbed away. Doubt, which was your ancient companion, has somehow crept back in through the doubt-flap. You could be master or mistress of the world but, like Alexander the Great, you are weeping because there are no more worlds to conquer. Welcome to the world of destination sickness.

Destination sickness is what my friend Christine was suffering from when she sat at her kitchen table and wept. She had a rich husband, a beautiful house and all the money and possessions she could want. Her adorable little daughter had started school that day and Christine sat down on her own and sobbed. 'There has to be more to life than this' is the thought that she sobbed through. And yet, a few years earlier, when she married, she had thought that perfect happiness came in the shape of a husband, home, children and wealth.

Destination sickness is the malady that infects you when you have arrived at the top of your world and find the joy seeping from you. The writer Lionel Shriver won a major book prize and described success and recognition as 'a quick high that fizzles'. She has learned that 'It's the stages before you get what you want that are the most enjoyable.'

The state you live in before you reach your destination is

not satisfying, but it is very alive. You are driven by longing and fantasy. Every possibility is exciting. You meet a new man and wonder if he could be the one. A need to prove yourself drives you in your work and your relationships. You burn with the injustices you want to correct.

It's essential to enjoy the process of achieving because achievement itself is an empty place which simply creates the space for another desire. I remember feeling intensely alive and excited when I was working for an MA. I loved the feeling of being stretched and stimulated and exhausted. When I'd finished, I was drained and flattened. 'Thank God' was instantly followed by 'Now what?' The fact that I now had two letters after my name didn't cancel out the sudden loss of focus and purpose.

Here's why everyone suffers from destination sickness

sooner or later. The only people who manage to avoid it are those who are afraid to pursue a dream and who turn their disappointment and irresolution into cynicism and despair. They choose a life of illusion over disillusion.

When you open the door to your dream home, whom do you find in it? Whose thoughts will you still be thinking as you wake up in your dream bedroom with your dream lover? When you walk off-stage with your mind and body vibrating with the ecstatic energy of a stadium full of fans, who will you end up with when the chauffeur leaves you at your door? Whose face will you see in the mirror? When, like Alexander the Great, you lead your men across a final frontier and realize that you've reached the furthest limits of your imagination, whose voice do you hear in your head and heart?

There is a great escape route from disillusion and that is that your goals and achievements are for other people, not yourself. If your destination somehow improves the common good, then that protects you from emptiness, but if you are after personal glory you will meet the inescapable you. You will be your own destination, no matter how far you travel.

The truth that you are your only destination is both good and bad news. It is bad news if you are floored by the fact that all the wealth and success in the world cannot protect you from the essential loneliness of the human condition. It cannot protect you from mortality either. What Alexander saw, over the rim of his last conquered world, was the irresistible figure of death.

However, it is very good news if you realize that you don't have to change the world around you in order to be happy.

Happiness is the invisible goal behind all the material trappings. People only want sex, money, power and possessions because they think they will be happy when they've got them. What if you cut out the middle men and went straight for the happiness? Wouldn't that save a lot of time and trouble? True happiness doesn't produce destination sickness. Instead it produces a feeling of contentment and profound gratitude.

Many studies have been done on happiness, and nobody has ever concluded that it depends on wealth and material success, not once the basic needs of life have been met. One definition of happiness that I read was Scottish country dancing. That was because it encompasses several aspects of happiness. It is sociable, and it makes you happy to do things with other people. It involves movement, and exercise makes you happy, especially exercise which is exhilarating. It involves music, which also lifts the spirits. And it involves learning something, which distracts and delights the brain.

Happiness, in my experience, depends greatly on paying attention to where you are and whom you are with now, rather than dreaming of some golden future. You can only get destination sickness if your happiness is dependent on reaching a destination. But there is no final resting-place in this world. The happiest people are those who are supremely interested in every step of the journey, no matter where it takes them.

Look on My Works,
Ye Mighty, and Despair

I'd like to take you on a journey to the ancient city of Balkh in northern Afghanistan. A wind is blowing across the steppes of Central Asia as you crunch over a vast level area of wasteland. High banks that must once upon a time have been city walls enclose a huge flat plain which is littered with broken stones and shards of pottery. Not one stone is left standing on another. Everything lies broken, in layers that go down over centuries.

Balkh is where history has been put through the blender of time and been pulverized. Two thousand years and more of human struggle, trading, fighting, conquest and habitation lie broken under your feet. Clues to the past are everywhere. Excavating, sorting, identifying, classifying, restoring the evidence of the changes of the past are the job of archaeologists. And yet, because of this constant process of change, very few archaeologists have ever been here long enough to make detailed sense of what this process of change has left behind.

Afghanistan has always stood at the crossroads of the world. 'You have the clocks,' Afghans are supposed to have jeered at each recent wave of invaders, 'but we have the time.'

They have aeons of time. Alexander the Great brought his conquering armies here and married an Afghan princess, Roxana. Genghis Khan and his Mongol hordes swept in from Central Asia, pulverizing everything under their horses' hooves. Tamburlaine followed him. So did the British, the Russians, the Taliban, the Americans. What has been salvaged from this wasteland of history may have been transferred to the museum in Kabul, where years of civil struggle and destruction would have damaged it still further.

The devastated landscape you look on is like the desert in

Shelley's poem *Ozymandias*. The poet finds a toppled statue of a king in the desert and the inscription on the statue reads:

> *'My name is Ozymandias, king of kings:*
> *Look on my works, ye Mighty, and despair!'*
> *Nothing beside remains. Round the decay*
> *Of that colossal wreck, boundless and bare*
> *The lone and level sands stretch far away.*

And yet something is still here. When I think of what overwhelming change means I often think of the landscape of Balkh. And when I think of what dogged survival means, for a nation, a people or for us as individuals, I think of Afghanistan.

What remains when everything seems to have been destroyed? What stays the same when everything seems to have changed? Something does. A name remains, and an idea. A history remains, and a narrative and people, and that history and that narrative give legitimacy and memory to the people, and that memory creates an identity, even when the stones are no longer standing. A sense of identity is hard to destroy and it can be rebuilt, which is why nations rise again from devastating wars and why people survive personal tragedies you would think might crush them.

When people look at the effects of change on their own lives they can often see that it is not success which defines them but the moments when they seemed to be surrounded by a wasteland. It is almost worth going through hard times in order to learn what spirit it gives you to come out as a survivor. You can guarantee that a roomful of people will rise to their feet to dance to *I Will Survive*, and they are not dancing out of self-pity but out of triumph and refusal to be put down.

We all need a sense of the past, but it is our sense of the future that drives and motivates us and gives us the courage to survive devastating change. We are far more than external things and material possessions. We are that entity which rebuilds on our own ruins and which runs up our own flag. The idea, whether it is an idea of a nation or an idea of our own identity, is more important than any trappings. The idea, the combination of history and vision, is where the energy is. With the right idea, the great and devastating change which seemed to sweep everything away will simply become incorporated into the irresistible momentum of our own story.

To Everything
There Is a Season

I thought winter would never end this year. Each cold morning I rose and raised my blinds and looked through the window to my left, to the flag flying on the church tower. If it strained stiffly towards the west I knew that the wind was still in the east. The wind from the east brings the breath of Siberia and the Russian steppes. It brings the bone-rattling chill of the North Sea. It scours the sky with cold clouds. Day after day I saw the evidence that the wind was in the east and some days I returned to bed, where it was warm, and I longed and longed for the wind to change. And the next morning I rose and looked again and it was Groundhog Day for me and the flag. The bloody wind was still in the bloody east.

On those endless icy days when I went out and gasped because the force and frigidity of the gusts at street corners took my breath away, I felt as though a spell had been cast over us.

Something in all of us longs for gentle progress. I grew desperate for signs of spring. I hunted for the tips of green shoots from spring bulbs. I could have gone down on my knees before the hope offered by the winter-flowering cherry trees that illuminated the dark streets. I gritted my teeth in a smile when friends jetted in from places where the sun shone and told me about their wonderful travels in Australia or Peru. Here in London we were stuck in Narnia, always winter, never Christmas. Christmas was behind us and the thaw of spring seemed unattainable.

It is spring now. The longed-for change has come. Dead trees and dead earth have begun to seethe with life. Magic has touched the city squares and gardens, and magnolias and cherry trees have burst into bloom. The Japanese, with their cherry-blossom-viewing parties, have the right reverence for transience. Perfection in a cherry tree is suspended for a single day of bud and bloom and then it rushes into blowsiness before it loses its head and its petals to the wind. For months I have been urging, 'Come on, come on,' and now I want to cry, 'Stop! Stop, while I look at you. Stop, because I haven't got time today, but I will come back and gaze tomorrow.' But tomorrow will not be the same.

Thank God I live in a country with seasons. Even though we curse and swear at rain and ice, every season has its own beauty and no day is ever the same. Today it was hot. It was the first hot day we've had this year and I went and lay on the grass with some friends, sharing our first picnic and feeling giddy about everything from the bluebells under the trees to the white clouds against the blue sky. We smeared on our first suntan lotion. We took off our shoes and felt the freshly cut grass under our feet. Everything about the day was precious because the weather had been so grim for so long. 'And tomorrow,' one of us said, 'it will be cold again and they've forecast rain.'

If every day were as gorgeous as today, no work would get done. And if every day were as cold and grey as February and March, we would want to emigrate. The art of living in a constantly changing climate is to give in to the joy of transience. When I look out over the May landscape I could eat the different greens I see – pinky green, acid lime, blue green, and all dusted with the puffs of wild cherry blossom. It will be gone in a week. The tide of dark green that sweeps in in June will blend all the trees together and only their shapes will give them away. And when the bronzes and russets and gold of the autumn have burned up the trees, I will be excited to see their true shapes return. Living in the country has taught me to love winter because it reveals the bone structure of nature. I am almost sorry when spring begins to blur the trees again.

When we are faced with beauty in one of its innumerable guises it is normal to want it to last forever. But the only things that last forever are inanimate. Life and its faces are fleeting. Art and photography try to arrest change, but living beauty can't be captured. The sunset you've saved on your computer is not the sunset you saw over the Pacific. Better to save the memory, because then you can add in the breeze on your skin and the crashing of the surf.

Really, transience is a blessing, because what is always before us becomes invisible. By constantly changing, life is constantly bringing itself to our attention. By constantly changing, it stimulates and demands a fresh response. By constantly changing, it forces us to adapt. By constantly changing, it forces us to live.

The Happy Ending

And now it is time for the happy ending. It is the end of the book and that is where the happy endings come. The dragon is slain. The prince and princess are living happily ever after. The wicked witch and the evil wizard are banished from the kingdom and we can all go to sleep.

Except that we can't. There are no real endings, only changes, transformations, mutations, intervals, transitions and endless new beginnings.

I remember rehearsing a requiem mass once with a conductor who had a good sense of humour. '*Requiem aeternam*,' he sang, with a twinkle in his eye. 'Eternal rest. Not for human beings.'

No, we are much luckier than that. We get the gift of life and its guarantee of change and restlessness. 'Eternal rest' is another phrase for death and we only long for death if life has somehow driven us to despair. If we are not desperate, everything in us clings to life, and no matter how challenging and difficult we find it, we value it so highly that we are driven, against all logic and common sense, to reproduce ourselves in order to hand this gift on.

I think that a huge part of the longing for children is the desire to introduce new human beings to everything we love about life. We want the joy of seeing them jump in puddles, of introducing them to the moon, the rainbow and the stars. We want to share the magic of snowflakes and the exhilaration of snowballs and toboggans and snowmen. We want our children to rekindle our own sense of discovery in reading our favourite stories, in exploring the summer beach or the autumn wood, in kicking a football or riding a bike. We want to rediscover our own passion for the unlimited, inexhaustible variety of life, of night and day, birds and beasts, imagination and play, reality and experiment.

One of the activities that everyone does with children is blowing bubbles. Another is blowing up balloons. Often babies cry when the beautiful bubble bursts and the magical balloon pops. And when they cry we laugh, not because we are cruel but because babies have to learn to take change lightly. Bubbles and balloons teach profound lessons. You create something exquisite and heartbreakingly transient. You marvel at it, you have no control over it, and then, pop, it's gone.

There are no happy endings because nothing really ends. There, the bubble has burst. But the idea and the possibility of bubbles still exist. As long as we have life we can blow more bubbles. There are glorious beginnings. And there are transcendental experiences. And there are magical encounters. Sometimes these encounters and experiences, like a great marriage or a wonderful career, last a lifetime, but within them they will encompass many, many changes and vicissitudes before death, the great change-master, brings them to an end.

And what of immortality? Nothing quite comes to an end. Life and death are the great recyclers. I caught my daughter having a dialogue with her dead grandfather. She was carrying round a big heavy book on politics. When I challenged her she said, 'It was Bill's book. I'm learning how Bill thought because when I get to a passage he underlined I stop and try to work out what he was thinking.'

My father may no longer be here on this Earth, but his mind is still interacting with the living. And his ashes are somewhere blowing on the wind, part of the global ecosystem. As for the energy that was his essential self, I don't have to believe in an afterlife to feel that somehow that is recycled too. It is part of the cosmic dance.

It can take a lifetime of experience and practice to learn to dance with change, but the rewards are huge. The sense of exhilaration that comes with change can be addictive. As for terrible changes, the ones that cluster under the headings of 'catastrophe' and 'disaster', they can also be ridden. Sadness and grief and loss are difficulties to be breathed in and moved through. They can be arduous changes of direction that call for new energy and motivation, but they need not be full stops.

No matter if something looks like an ending, happy or sad, it too will pass. So, keep moving. Keep the sense of a bigger pattern. Don't take it personally. Bow to the laws of impermanence and tune in to their rhythm. Give thanks for the magical, mischievous ride we are all on. And above all, keep breathing.

Resources

Change is a huge subject. You can do whole degrees in change management. The business management shelves in libraries and bookshops are stuffed with tomes about change. So is the self-help section. You can't turn on a television without finding programmes about changing your appearance, your house, the country you live in or your finances. A lot of the books are unreadable and a lot of the television programmes are superficial, but the messages from all these sources are universal: Change is possible. You don't have to be stuck. Change is difficult, but it can be managed. Change, like every other aspect of life, can be studied and understood.

I am not going to suggest any of these management books because they are not the only guides to change and they are no fun to read. You'll learn more about social and political change by reading books on history and politics and philosophy. You'll learn more about how people change through reading great novels, going to good plays and going to the movies. Go to museums and art galleries and tell yourself, 'I'm here to learn about change,' and you will be surprised what that brings into focus for you.

In this book I have mentioned one or two writers. Sigmund Freud was a wonderful lucid writer as well as the founder of psychoanalysis. Stifled creatives always enjoy reading and doing the exercises in Julia Cameron's book *The Artist's Way* (Souvenir Press, 1994).

I have also mentioned the Hoffman Process, a week-long course which has galvanized thousands of people into changing their future by confronting and coming to terms with their past. You can learn more about them on www.hoffmaninstitute.co.uk or by reading Tim Laurence's book *You Can Change your Life* (Hodder & Stoughton, 2003).

What I've learned in writing this book is that change is more of an experience than a theory. If you want to learn about change, do something different and see what happens. It could be fun.

If you enjoyed this book you may like to know that Lesley Garner has published two previous books: *Everything I've Ever Done That Worked* and *Everything I've Ever Learned About Love*. Both these books are available from all good book shops or by calling Hay House Publishers direct on 020 8962 1230.

Everything I've Ever Done That Worked

Distilled from Lesley's own resource book, the one she wrote for herself from 30 years of taking notes and writing articles and diaries. Lesley wrote it because just when she thinks she knows what to do life bowls her over again and she forgets what's worked. This is Lesley's own spiritual and emotional first aid kit. It holds things that work in darkness and things that work in daylight. There are techniques that will help you plan your journey and techniques that will light the next inch of the path when you've lost your way. They give comfort in a crisis but they'll also inspire you to lead a deeper, richer life.

Everything I've Ever Learned About Love

Everyone who reads this book will find their idea of love expanded and transformed. Through the prism of her own life, Lesley Garner reflects on the love of family, lovers, children, parents, friends, work, nature, art and landscape. She celebrates all love's moods, from agony to ecstasy, despair to joy. This is a book about her, but it is also a book about you. Read it and your awareness of love will be changed for ever.

HAY HOUSE PUBLISHERS

Your Essential Life Companions

For the most up-to-date
information on the
latest releases, author
appearances and a host
of special offers, visit

www.hayhouse.co.uk

Tune into **www.hayhouseradio.com**
to hear inspiring live radio shows daily!

292B Kensal Rd, London W10 5BE
Tel: 020 8962 1230 Email: info@hayhouse.co.uk

We hope you enjoyed this Hay House book.
If you would like to receive a free catalogue featuring additional
Hay House books and products, or if you would like information
about the Hay Foundation, please contact:

Hay House UK Ltd

292B Kensal Rd • London W10 5BE
Tel: (44) 20 8962 1230; Fax: (44) 20 8962 1239
www.hayhouse.co.uk

✳✳✳

Published and distributed in the United States of America by:
Hay House, Inc. • PO Box 5100 • Carlsbad, CA 92018-5100
Tel: (1) 760 431 7695 or (800) 654 5126;
Fax: (1) 760 431 6948 or (800) 650 5115
www.hayhouse.com

Published and distributed in Australia by:
Hay House Australia Ltd • 18/36 Ralph St • Alexandria NSW 2015
Tel: (61) 2 9669 4299 • Fax: (61) 2 9669 4144
www.hayhouse.com.au

Published and distributed in the Republic of South Africa by:
Hay House SA (Pty) Ltd • PO Box 990 • Witkoppen 2068
Tel/Fax: (27) 11 706 6612 • orders@psdprom.co.za

Distributed in Canada by:
Raincoast • 9050 Shaughnessy St • Vancouver, BC V6P 6E5
Tel: (1) 604 323 7100 • Fax: (1) 604 323 2600

✳✳✳

Sign up via the Hay House UK website to receive the Hay House
online newsletter and stay informed about what's going on with
your favourite authors. You'll receive bimonthly announcements
about discounts and offers, special events, product highlights,
free excerpts, giveaways, and more!
www.hayhouse.co.uk